LOOKING AT ART
IN THE CLASSROOM

Art Investigations from the Guggenheim Museum

REBECCA SHULMAN HERZ

FOREWORD BY GRANT WIGGINS

TEACHERS COLLEGE PRESS

Teachers College, Columbia University
New York and London

Published by Teachers College Press, 1234 Amsterdam Avenue, New York, NY 10027

The work reported in this volume was supported by: Federal Grant #U351D060059 and U.S. Department of Education grant #U351D03009905. Any opinions, findings, conclusions, or recommendations expressed herein are those of the Author and do not necessarily reflect the views or policies of the funding agency.

Library of Congress Cataloging-in-Publication Data
Herz, Rebecca Shulman.
  Looking at art in the classroom : art investigations from the Guggenheim Museum / Rebecca Shulman Herz.
    p. cm.
  Includes bibliographical references and index.
  ISBN 978-0-8077-5047-6 (pbk. : alk. paper)
  1. Art—Study and teaching (Elementary) 2. Art and society. I. Solomon R. Guggenheim Museum. II. Title.
  LB1592.H47 2010
    372.5—dc22

                                                                2009031657

ISBN 978-0-8077-5047-6 (paper)

Printed on acid-free paper
Manufactured in the United States of America

17 16 15 14 13 12 11 10   8 7 6 5 4 3 2 1

For Alex, Charlotte, and Nathaniel

CONTENTS

FOREWORD

IT IS RARE in education for a book to delight, provoke, and help the reader all at once. This text does all three with clarity, style, and purpose—like a good work of art.

Any time educators venture into areas out of our comfort zone we run the risk of backtracking quickly in fear of looking foolish and feeling out of control; we all too easily turn our backs on a new approach, even a highly promising one, out of discomfort. This wonderful book not only will help all teachers—regardless of prior experience—feel immediately comfortable teaching about and through art, it will help *any* educator understand better how to teach for student understanding and engagement—regardless of subject matter.

The text contains all a teacher needs to know about how to develop thematic, in-depth, and engaging work for students. The reader will not only become increasingly competent but confident in facilitating inquiry into meaningful issues through the lens of real works of art. In the end, there is a double satisfaction: One becomes not only a better teacher but a better researcher into one's own craft and develops questions by following the process outlined.

Of great value here is the ease with which the Art Investigation Methodology framing of artistic inquiry permits easy integration with work in other subject areas. By identifying powerful themes, corresponding questions, and illustrative works of art, any teacher will easily see new and exciting possibilities for coherent instruction across different subjects. In short, the methodology described here will make it far more likely that teachers become more focused and in-depth in all their unit-design work.

In these times—where far too many timid faculties have retreated to reading,'riting, and 'rithmetic over accountability worries—it is an absolute pleasure to read a book that not only stands proud in support of the arts, but holds out a shining example for all other subjects on how to teach for in-depth and meaningful understanding.

The Art Investigation Methodology, in short, has intrinsic power and practical transfer ability. What more can we ask of an innovation in education?

—Grant Wiggins

ACKNOWLEDGMENTS

PERHAPS SOME BOOKS are written in solitude and go directly from author to publisher. Not this one. Many people contributed to the development, writing, and refinement of this book.

Kim Kanatani, the Gail Engelberg Director of Education at the Guggenheim Museum, arrived at the museum in 2001 with clear and practical ideas about what inquiry with art should look like, which have guided the Guggenheim's education department in developing and refining the Art Investigation Methodology. A team of extraordinary teaching artists practiced and helped refine this methodology, as well as developing practices in art making that are referenced throughout this book; this team includes Kate Baird, Jenny Bevill, Jen Cecere, Ascha Kells Drake, Mark Dzula, Emily Gibson, Ardina Greco, Jeff Hopkins, Emily Lambert, Susan Mayr, Mollie McQuarrie, Kristin Melin, Anette Millington, Antonia Perez, and James Reynolds.

The Art Investigations featured in this book were adapted from real conversations led by classroom teachers and teaching artists trained by the Guggenheim Museum in this methodology. These classroom teachers were brave and creative in implementing this methodology in their classroom: thanks to Denise Hughes, Ivelisses Molina, Jennifer Sussman, Lynnette Deane, Katy Vicchito, and Christie Paul.

Guggenheim Museum colleagues Sharon Vatsky, Associate Director for School Programs, and Jacklyn Delamatre, former Education Program Coordinator, helped to guide the research that led to this book and then to conceptualize this book. As the contents were identified and the book took shape, more colleagues helped with research, writing, and editing. Educators Amy Charleroy, Mayrav Fisher, Stacy Fisher, Chelsea Frosini, Marie Reilly Levenick, Miriam Leviton, and Tracy Truels, along with Jacklyn Delamatre and Sharon Vatsky, edited each chapter at various stages. Curators Tracey Bashkoff, Megan Fontanella, and Nancy Spector ensured the integrity of all art historical statements. Sharon Dively secured the images and permissions.

Olga Hubard, assistant professor of art education at Columbia University Teachers College, and Anne Rhodes, art education consultant, generously made time to read each chapter carefully, sharing feedback that greatly improved the book.

The Guggenheim is tremendously grateful to the United States Department of Education for leadership support of this project. In addition, special thanks go to the following for key funding of Learning Through Art: Citi Foundation, Horace W. Goldsmith Foundation, The Seth Sprague Educational and Charitable Foundation, New York City Department of Cultural Affairs, and New York State Council on the Arts. Major endowment and operating support of general education programming at the Guggenheim has also been provided by The Edith and Frances Mulhall Achilles Memorial Fund, The Engelberg Foundation, William Randolph Hearst Foundation, Mortimer D. Sackler Family, The Peter Jay Sharp Foundation, and members of the Museum's Education Committee.

INTRODUCTION

WHY DO SOME PEOPLE enjoy looking at art, while others are baffled or bored? How do we become people who derive enjoyment from art, and how do we offer this to our students? How do we learn to look carefully and persistently, so that a work of art continues to offer us new surprises? How do we learn to revel in the associations that our minds offer us, make guesses about what we are seeing, and surprise ourselves with new ideas about or connections to a work of art?

One of the goals of art museum education is to engage visitors in experiences with art that are surprising and memorable—experiences that involve looking, associating, and analyzing. Inquiry-based museum education approaches are rooted in constructivist educational methodology, which holds that individuals do not learn by memorizing a static body of knowledge, but rather by creating new meanings through the intersection of what they already know and believe with new ideas and knowledge. For the educator engaging students with art, this implies that students need opportunities to connect existing ideas and knowledge with the work in front of them, and to make their own meanings from these connections. The Guggenheim Museum's Art Investigation Methodology is an example of this inquiry-based approach.

This book was written with the goal of sharing the Art Investigation Methodology with classroom teachers, both of art and of other subjects. Art Investigations pose questions that engage students in careful observation and interpretation of a work of art. Questions are crafted to help students contextualize the work of art within a theme that relates to both the work of art and the larger work of the classroom. Information is shared in order to further students' ability to interpret a work of art for themselves, or in order to answer questions that they have posed. Follow-up prompts and questions help students go deeper into their understanding of the art, making connections between their ideas and what they are seeing. While the teaching strategies shared in this volume can be adapted for use with any age group, this book specifically addresses the teaching of students in second through eighth grades.

In observing and sharing interpretations of a work of art, students practice attention to detail, inference, and the ability to consider multiple perspectives—skills also needed to analyze a work of literature or a historical document. Art Investigations promote curiosity, a willingness to puzzle through a question or problem, and the ability to hypothesize and give evidence—skills highly valued in both science and mathematics. During Art Investigations students think for themselves as well as listen to others—essential skills for independent thinkers and citizens of a democracy. Additionally, engaging collectively in Art Investigations can build community in the classroom, as students work collaboratively to make meaning and learn more about one another, while sharing opinions in a supportive environment.

For the non-art teacher, Art Investigations can provide an exciting way to examine contemporary and historical cultures. They also engage students in considering how artists respond to issues relevant to the classroom: What does it mean to be human? How do we create and maintain community? How do citizens of the twenty-first century relate to the natural world? Imagine the richness added to a unit on societal changes caused by the Industrial Revolution by looking at Camille Pissarro's painting Hermitage at Pontoise (Plate 14), or the possibilities opened up by including Louise Bourgeoise's deeply autobiographical sculptures (Plate 15) in a unit on metaphor.

For the art teacher, Art Investigations help students genuinely explore the work that artists do: both the techniques artists use and the ways of thinking that go into creating a work of art. Looking at art is an important aspect of developing an artistic practice. Artists look at other artists' work for inspiration and also as members of a shared community. Artists revisit certain artworks and the work of certain artists over and over, because they like them or are intrigued by them and because they learn from them. Often the work of one artist is immensely inspirational: The photographer Catherine Opie knew she wanted to be a photographer from the time she wrote a school report about the work of photographer Lewis Hine. Artists think independently, imaginatively, and critically about the artwork they look at, wondering how the artist manipulated his or her materials, considering what the artist might have been trying to say, and comparing one work of art to another. Art Investigations provide the tools to engage students meaningfully with the world of art and artists.

MUSEUM EDUCATORS HAVE long claimed that audiences build critical thinking skills through inquiry-based discussions about art and objects. In 2003, the Guggenheim Museum began to investigate the accuracy of this assertion. In that year, the Guggenheim was awarded a United States Department of Education grant to conduct research to examine whether Art Investigation

Methodology cultivated critical thinking skills and whether these skills might transfer to other subject areas. Because of the similarities between literature and art, as well as the current educational emphasis on literacy skills, the research looked at whether critical thinking skills transferred to the area of English language arts. Could Art Investigations help students learn to think more critically not only about visual art but also about written texts?

The context for this research, and for the refinement of the Art Investigation Methodology, was the Guggenheim Museum's Learning Through Art program. Learning Through Art (LTA) was founded in 1970, at a time when schools in New York City were losing their arts programs due to budget cuts. Founder Natalie Lieberman saw the program as a literacy intervention, as well as a way to keep the arts in public schools. LTA sends teaching artists into New York City classrooms, where they collaborate with classroom teachers to develop projects that explore ideas related to the school curriculum. These residencies are extensive: Most include 20 classroom sessions and three museum visits, offering participating students a significant amount of art instruction throughout the year.

The primary focus of LTA is on making art, rather than looking at it. However, students participating in the program also look at art in every session with teaching artists. They look at art to consider both art technique and curriculum-related ideas, and they understand that looking at art is an important part of their role as artists and researchers. Each of these conversations around works of art is facilitated using the Art Investigation Methodology. While at first teachers were concerned that students would be fidgety and bored as they waited to make art, they quickly found that students love Art Investigations. When a teaching artist displays a poster or projects an image for students, hands fly into the air; the students are eager to share what they notice. When teaching artists ask students to analyze works of art, the answers are thoughtful and often surprising. A community of art viewers, art appreciators, and critical thinkers develops.

The repeated use of Art Investigation Methodology in Learning Through Art classrooms offered a laboratory in which the Guggenheim could examine the impact of this method over an extended period of time. Working with the evaluation firm Randi Korn and Associates, along with an advisory team of literacy and art specialists, the Guggenheim took 3 years to plan and conduct a quantitative and rigorous research study. The study found that the Learning Through Art program did indeed produce students who were better able to think critically when looking at works of art and when reading texts than their peers. Teachers, teaching artists, and program advisers attribute these findings to students' frequent participation in Art Investigations.

This book outlines the Art Investigation Methodology, its applications in the art and non-art classrooms, and the impact of Art Investigations on specific critical thinking skills. Chapter 1 addresses a series of questions: Why look at art in the classroom? Why use this inquiry-based methodology? Why do this as a classroom community? Chapters 2 and 3 outline basic techniques for how to write an Art Investigation plan and how to lead an Art Investigation in the classroom. Chapter 4 considers the use of this methodology within the art classroom; Chapter 5 considers the role of Art Investigations in an integrated curriculum. Chapter 6 outlines the impact of Art Investigations on critical thinking and literacy skills.

Introducing art into the classroom offers students access to one of the great areas of human achievement. The goal of an Art Investigation is to teach students to look at art the way artists do: to become independent and confident viewers and meaning makers. People who view art this way look carefully, think critically, are curious about and understand something about the world beyond their own experience, and have language for describing the world. To become careful observers, critical thinkers, and curious learners: isn't that what we wish for all of our children?

Chapter 1

ART INVESTIGATION METHODOLOGY: AN OVERVIEW

A GROUP OF fifth-grade students sits in front of a poster depicting ballet dancers (Plate 1). Hands are raised, even though the teacher has not yet asked a question. The teacher makes a motion indicating that they should put their hands down, and says, "Take a couple of minutes and look carefully at this painting. What do you notice?" The students look carefully for a few minutes, and then the hands creep back into the air, and the teacher begins to call on individual students.

"It looks like ballerinas that are going on stage."

"What makes you say that they are about to go on stage?" asks the teacher.

"Because on one side it looks like the fitting room and backstage, and on the other side there's lots of colors and the background."

"I notice that their skirts are only green and yellow," shares another student.

A classmate adds, "I also think they're going to go on stage soon, because usually when someone goes on stage they kind of look a little nervous, and it looks like some of them are doing stretches."

"What makes you think they're nervous?" prompts the teacher.

"Because they're clumped together."

The child sitting nearby volunteers, "The curtain is in front of them, and it looks like they're getting ready to dance."

Another classmate chimes in, "The dancer in the back is kind of peeking over, like she's really nervous."

A student near the back says, "I also notice that at the bottom where their feet are you can also see the shadows, and it looks like there's a little wheel in the back near the legs."

"What do you think that wheel might be?" the teacher asks.

"I think that wheel . . . I see the wall, and then something that might be the background for the thing that they might dance to, which kind of looks like nature, and the wheel is part of that to help move it."

The teacher nods. "It sounds like you're saying that this is part of the *stage set*. Do you all know that term? The things that come in and out, on and off the stage."

"I also notice that they're barefoot, and they don't look like they're wearing slippers."

"It's a little bit hard to tell because of the way the artist is making the marks, so if they are wearing slippers, the slippers might be the same pink color as their skin," says the teacher, adding a slight correction to the student's statement, while validating the observation. The teacher goes on to give the students some information. "The artist is named Edgar Degas, and he was painting in a time period when some artists were interested in showing moments from everyday life. So Degas is showing these dancers backstage, instead of onstage. What do you think is interesting to Degas about these dancers backstage?"

"Maybe their curiosity."

"Maybe people could think about what the dancers are thinking about."

"What do you think they're thinking about?" asks the teacher.

"Things they should do to make their performance better."

"They're probably thinking about how the audience feels about the performance."

"I have a question," says one child. "What is the painting called?"

"*Dancers in Green and Yellow*," answers the teacher. "Someone here noticed that their skirts are green and yellow."

"I think they might be thinking about whether they're going to be better than the people who are already on stage."

"Great. I want to go back to the question we've been wondering about in class lately, which is how artists and writers influence the world, and how their thinking changes our thinking. What are some ideas you have for how Degas might have wanted to change how people thought?"

"It's not all about what happens on stage, things also happen offstage."

"Maybe the people who watch the dances don't know how scary it is right before you perform, and what the dancers are going through."

"Those are some great ideas for how an artist might paint something to make us think in new ways. Great work," says the teacher.

THE ABOVE DIALOGUE is adapted from an Art Investigation led by a Guggenheim Museum teaching artist. *Art Investigation Methodology* is an inquiry-based practice of looking at and discussing art. There is a wide range of methodologies educators use to look at art with students, developed and honed by museum educators and art educators over the past few decades. Some are defined by a standardized series of questions, focusing on building critical thinking skills.[1] Others reject questions in favor of provocative statements that jump-start conversation, and encourage looking at a single object for as long as one hour.[2] Yet others intersperse questions and information, using student answers as a jumping-off point for teaching students about a specific work of art.

The Art Investigation Methodology uses questions to engage viewers with a work of art for a 10–20 minute experience focused on a specific theme, identified in advance by the teacher. It assumes that information helps to deepen one's understanding of an artwork, but the ultimate goal of these conversations is less to learn in depth about a specific work of art than to learn how to look at and make sense of art more generally.

Art Investigations are best used with students who are in second grade or above, who are developmentally ready to make and defend hypotheses and to understand the point of view of others. Younger students get very excited about looking at art and sharing their observations. They like to identify or name things, to categorize, and to relate what they are seeing to their own experiences. They also like to listen to stories about art. However, it is often difficult for them to engage as a group in the interpretive work of delving deeper.

The Art Investigation Methodology is a practical approach in that it recognizes the limits of both the teacher's time for learning about a work of art in advance, and the time available in a classroom or museum for looking at a single work of art. Because it is theme-based, it is easy to link to other areas of investigation throughout the curriculum.

To prepare for leading an Art Investigation, the teacher develops three to five open-ended questions, beginning with questions that invite students to make observations, and then moving into questions that ask for interpretations of the artwork, as well as asking students to make connections between the art and their own lives or other areas of study. Each question posed by the teacher is followed by time for students to give a variety of answers. When they interpret the artwork, students are asked to back up their ideas with evidence from the artwork. Information is offered at critical points during the conversation, in such a way that it helps students build their own understandings of the artwork. In an expertly led Art Investigation, the students are each thinking independently, and the conversation results in ideas and interpretations that the teacher could not have predicted in advance.

This methodology—indeed, this book—begs the questions: Why look at art with students? Why look at art using an inquiry-based methodology? Why do this in a group setting? What are the goals and benefits of this particular approach? Why should Art Investigations be of interest to classroom teachers?

WHY LOOK AT ART WITH STUDENTS?

There are many reasons to look at art. Art is compelling, and engaging. Art is multilayered and ambiguous, open to interpretation. It is rich with emotion and often evokes a responding emotion in the viewer. Art is often beautiful, and beauty offers pleasure; when it is not beautiful, it is generally purposefully not beautiful, engaging us in important questions about what we choose to look at and how we respond. Art is an important part of what humanity has produced, from cave dwellers 30,000 years ago through to today.

For the classroom teacher focused on creating lessons that further curricular and skill-based learning goals, there are at least two important reasons to look at art in the classroom. The first is that art is an important form of communication and therefore communicates important information about people, times, and places. The second is that art teaches us about the imagination, a critical human ability. These two reasons for looking at art are discussed at length below.

Art Is a Form of Communication

Often artists communicate personal reactions to the world. Pablo Picasso purposefully shared his understanding of the horrors of war and, perhaps less purposefully, his ideas about women. These themes might evoke terror, sympathy, repulsion, longing, intellectual concern, or some other response in the viewer. In evoking these reactions, art engages us with the shared concerns of humanity.

Sometimes art captures societal concerns or changes. For example, Western European Impressionist artists documented the social and industrial changes of the late nineteenth century. Smog from factories is visible in some paintings; others focus on the new leisure pursuits of the urban middle class. Some artists address societal ideas about the role of women, particularly the role of working women. A different societal change is captured in Medieval and Renaissance art depicting children: These paintings reveal, to various degrees, a conception of children as smaller adults. In looking at this art we begin to understand that hundreds of years ago childhood was not understood in the way that we see it now.

Often functional objects such as vessels, tools, or weapons communicate information about a culture. An Aztec brazier (a container for fire) featuring three accordioned human faces conveys information about Aztec ideas related to stages of life, aging, and dying (Solis, 2004, p. 7; see Figure 1.1). A Maori feather box decorated with faces of ancestors represents both the importance of ancestors and the belief that a chief was so sacred that anything

Figure 1.1. *Fragment of a Brazier: Three Ages*
Aztec, ca. 1300
Clay and pigment
18 x 22 x 9 cm
Museo Nacional de Antropologia e Historia, Mexico City, D. F., Mexico

that touched his head became sacred (Burn, 1993, p. 277; see Figure 1.2). One could argue that the study of any culture or era is incomplete without taking into account the art produced during that time, in that place.

Information about a time period, culture, or artist is often not readily apparent to the novice or uninformed viewer. Art historians rely upon information from myriad sources to decipher the cultural relevance and information within any work of art. Information that is not found in the physical work of art itself is often critical to a deep and accurate understanding of the work. It is this combination of information brought in from other sources and the careful observation and interpretation of the work of art itself that leads to depth and accuracy of understanding of both the work of art and the artist or culture that created it.

As viewers, we learn about individuals, communities, and cultures by viewing their art. We also learn about the tools of visual communication: how symbolism can be used to convey an emotion or an idea; how color or brushstroke

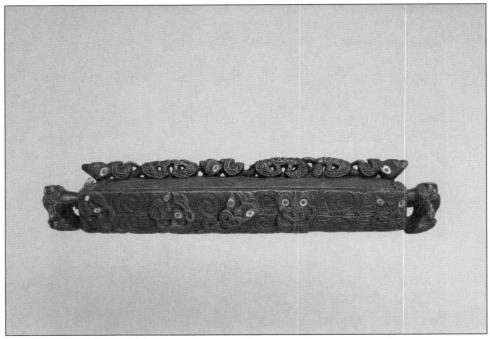

Figure 1.2. *Treasure Box (Papahou)*
New Zealand (Aotearoa), Maori, Bay of Plenty, 18th century
Wood, shell
L: 17 5/8 inches (44.8 cm)
The Metropolitan Museum of Art
The Michael C. Rockefeller Memorial Collection, Purchase, Nelson A. Rockefeller Gift,
1960 (1978.412.755 a, b)

can be expressive; how we react differently to a photograph than to a drawing. Understanding the ways an image can evoke a response is particularly important in the twenty-first century, where we are inundated with images, many of which are being used to try and sell us a product or an idea. In understanding the ways that art communicates, the viewer also comes to understand the role of the artist in society as someone with an interest in and commitment to sharing his or her perceptions of and responses to the world.

Art Engages the Imagination

Art helps us contemplate the "what ifs" of the world, the worlds beyond the everyday world. Artists work in the realm of the imagination. They contemplate the world as something other than its most obvious physical manifestation, whether by reimagining a landscape to perfect a composition or by imagining an entirely new world. By engaging with art, we learn to consider the "what ifs" ourselves, the process of imagining the world as something other than what it is or what it seems to be: What would the world look like if you could see string theory at work? What is the loneliest scene you can imagine? If we could create the ideal world, what would it look like? What if we changed the rules of art itself? This capacity for imagination is part of what makes us human. It is what enables us to act upon and make changes to the world we live in, whether as an artist, a politician, a teacher, or a practitioner in some career not yet dreamed of.

One of the "what ifs" the arts help us to explore is the "what if" of other people's experiences. Art helps us to learn about the lives of others, empathizing and feeling sympathy and concern where we might previously have been unfeeling. George Eliot (1856/1963) wrote:

> The greatest benefit we owe to the artist, whether painter, poet, or novelist, is the extension of our sympathies. . . . [For example] when Hornung paints a group of chimney-sweepers,—more is done towards linking the higher classes with the lower, towards obliterating the vulgarity of exclusiveness, than by hundreds of sermons and philosophical dissertations. Art is the nearest thing to life; it is a mode of amplifying experience and extending our contact with our fellow-men beyond the bounds of our personal lot. (pp. 270–271)

In the Art Investigation that begins this chapter, students contemplated the experience of dancers waiting backstage. Many of them thought that the dancers might be nervous, drawing on their understanding of both the situation—waiting to go onstage before an audience—and the body language depicted: "they're clumped together," noted one student. When asked what they might be thinking about, students indicated not only that they understood how the dancers felt, but that the audience might not: "Maybe the people who watch the dancers don't know how scary it is right before you perform, and what the dancers are going through."

WHY ENGAGE IN INQUIRY AROUND ART?

There are many ways to look at and make sense of a work of art. You can view it silently, perhaps sketching or writing notes, or just quietly appreciating. You can attend a lecture, learning about the contexts of a work of art as well as the ways that art historians and critics have interpreted the work. You might read a book or watch a movie about the artist. What are the advantages of pairing an inquiry-based methodology with the experience of art viewing? Note that the word *inquiry* is used to describe many different (although related) educational methodologies. Here we will define it as a teaching strategy in which the teacher poses open-ended observation and interpretation questions about a work of art, and the conversation grows naturally out of these questions.

Terry Barrett (2003) writes: "Works of art are mere things until we begin to carefully perceive and interpret them—then they become alive and enliven us as we reflect on, wonder about, and respond to them" (p. xv). Inquiry engages students in the rich mysteries of art and offers them the opportunity to understand how deep, confusing, ambiguous, multilayered, and wonderful a work of art can be, and to become expert in the act of art viewing. In the process of engaging in inquiry, students also build their abilities in four areas: First, the inquiry teaches the tools of the art historian. Second, inquiry encourages connections and personal meaning making. Third, inquiry teaches curiosity. And fourth, inquiry cultivates critical thinking skills. While all but the first of these abilities can be honed by using inquiry in other contexts, art provides a fertile, layered context that easily and genuinely lends itself to ongoing inquiry.

Inquiry Teaches the Tools of the Art Historian

Careful observation followed by interpretation is the process that art historians and critics follow. By engaging students in this work, teachers give them the tools of the discipline. Rather than focusing on learning information about particular works of art, they are learning how to make sense of art for themselves. This is a portable tool, and one that will help students engage with art in a meaningful way beyond the classroom setting.

Works of art are ambiguous, layered things that cannot be explained in a straightforward way or fully interpreted by one person for another. Art historians often disagree on their interpretation of a work of art. They are interested in, look for, and make connections between different things. One art historian might look at Marc Chagall's painting *Paris Through the Window* (Plate 2) and notice his fantastical view of the world; another might attend to his debt to the ways his contemporary, Robert Delaunay, painted Paris; and yet another might interpret the painting as an emotional tribute to his immigrant status, with a love of Paris and roots in Russia. Inquiry allows students this same experience of attending to what interests them and forming individual interpretations.

Inquiry Encourages Connections and Personal Meaning Making

As inquiry helps students become sophisticated and independent art viewers, it also allows learners to find or create their own meaning in a work of art. When investigating a work of art through open-ended questions, students are free to identify what they notice in a work of art—what calls out to them when they first see it, and what happens when they continue looking. Each student might notice something different. In the Art Investigation of *Dancers in Green and Yellow* (related above), one student is interested in the narrative ("It looks like ballerinas that are going on stage") and another in the colors ("their skirts are only green and yellow"). Later in the conversation one student attends to the actions of the figures (noticing that they are doing stretches and are "clumped together") and another to the theatrical equipment ("there's a little wheel in the back near the legs"). The students attend to what interests them, from which they can later make communal or individual sense.

Students are offered the opportunity both to interpret a work of art in the context of their own experience and then to move beyond their own experience. For example, the fifth-grade students featured in the conversation that opened this chapter are clearly considering their own experiences onstage, or understandings of what it might be like to be onstage, as they discuss Edgar Degas's *Dancers in Green and Yellow*. These comparisons allow students to place the work of art within a known context. Later, information or observations might reveal differences as well, opening up the world of new experiences and new meanings.

Inquiry allows students to make connections both implicitly and explicitly, making the investigation of a work of art more meaningful than it might be in a lecture setting. It also teaches students to make connections between the new and the known, considering new images, ideas, and information in light of their existing knowledge and concerns. This is an empowering way of approaching anything new, and helps students become self-guided learners in charge of their own education.

The observations and connection making of an inquiry lead to a student-crafted interpretation of the work. This interpretation (e.g., that the artist appears to be interested in what the dancers are thinking about) may be similar to what thousands have thought previously, or it may be unique to this conversation. Students are working within constraints: they are challenged to craft defensible interpretations that make sense related to what they see, as well as what they know about the work of art and its context. Within these constraints, however, students are empowered to create meaning. After learning how to conduct Art Investigations in her classroom, one teacher reported in her workshop evaluation, "It has allowed my students to take ownership of their ideas." Opportunities for active meaning making in the classroom help students assign personal importance to their own theories and observations.

Inquiry Teaches Curiosity

Inquiry is rooted in open-ended questions, questions which merit real attention. Through this format, inquiry models curiosity. It offers students questions that genuinely challenge them to wonder about the world ("How do artists and writers influence the world?"). It models questions that adults ask and ponder ("What do you think is interesting to Degas about these dancers backstage?"), demonstrating the power of a good question to capture the imagination and continue calling to the learner after the lesson is over. It also provides a space in which students can formulate and pose their own questions ("Maybe people could think about what the dancers are thinking about") and engage their classmates in helping to explore and address these questions.

Inquiry not only poses questions, it explores possible answers and allows these answers to be generated by the students. Students rarely pose or engage meaningfully with questions if they do not believe that they can make progress toward finding an answer to the question. Therefore, an important facet of curiosity is students' beliefs that they can find a meaningful answer to the question. Through inquiry, question posing and question answering become the work we do together as an academic community.

Inquiry Cultivates Critical Thinking Skills

Inquiry also teaches *critical thinking skills,* a vague and much-used term that we will define here as the ability to put forth an interpretation or understanding of something and to evaluate interpretations or understandings. Thinking critically requires that people not only put forth debatable statements or ideas, but also understand why they think these statements or ideas are valid, attending to the question, "How do I know this?" (Felton & Kuhn, 2007). A number of skills taught in the classroom are rooted in critical thinking, including reading comprehension (understanding what you read), the scientific method (putting forth hypotheses and evaluating them), and essay writing (positing an idea and arguing for it). Mature critical thinkers understand that more than one interpretation can be correct, that some ideas are better than others, and that understanding how someone knows something and why he or she thinks it to be true is essential to judging the accuracy of an idea (Felton & Kuhn, 2007).

Critical thinking skills are essential to successful adults, who must be able to know when they agree or disagree with a neighbor or a politician and to accept or reject the arguments put forth in advertisements or newspaper articles. A salesperson's task is to figure out what products might be best suited for a specific customer; a police officer must be able to determine when they think someone poses a threat and why they think this to be so; a doctor must decide what might be ailing a patient; a magazine editor is charged with selecting articles that are relevant to the magazine's audience. To do any of these jobs well requires complex critical thinking skills.

Critical thinking skills are often taught by looking at and analyzing texts. However, for the child who is struggling to decode written language or simply dislikes reading, the text itself poses a barrier to learning the more global thinking skills. For many students, it is useful to build these skills in contexts that do not involve the written word. Visual images are useful starting points for classroom discussions in part because they do not demand a learned skill, such as alphabetic decoding, to interpret. In addition, they provide an immediately accessible, fully apparent shared referent; the entire class can view a poster of a work of art together, taking in the scope of the piece simply by looking at it. Whereas in analyzing a text one might need to flip through pages to find a quote to support a hypothesis or skim through paragraphs to find a specific passage, with many works of art the evidence is in front of the entire class, ready to be referred to and jointly analyzed.

A group of second graders discussing Faith Ringgold's story quilt *Tar Beach* (Plate 3) illustrate the development of critical thinking skills during an Art Investigation. When the teacher asked, "What can we guess about what's happening in this picture?" students shared a variety of answers.

"They're looking up at the stars."

"They're eating."

"It might be too cold."

To challenge this student to think more carefully about his hypothesis that it was cold out, the teacher followed up by asking, "Why do you think it might be cold?"

The child paused for a moment to look carefully at the artwork, then said, "I disagree with my own self. I don't think they're cold, because they're wearing skirts and short sleeves and no socks and shoes."

Later, the students worked together to understand how two of the figures seem to be sleeping on the roof. One child stated, "I think they're crazy because they brought their bed up on the roof."

"I don't think that's a bed; that's just a mattress," suggested another student.

The teacher looked at the image and then asked, "Does anyone else have any thoughts about this?"

A third child said, "I agree that they're up on the roof, but I don't think that's a bed or a mattress, I think it's just a blanket or a mat they're lying on so that when they're sleepy they don't have to go all the way downstairs to bed and then forget to say something and come back up."

Instead of being told that the artwork depicts a hot summer night, with two children asleep on blankets on the roof, the students were working hard to examine the available evidence, and to form and share hypotheses about the scene before them. The openness of the inquiry-based format allowed them to look more closely, to think more carefully, and to change their minds. It is a slow way to get information, but an excellent way to learn how to think.

WHY ENGAGE IN INQUIRY
AROUND ART AS A CLASSROOM COMMUNITY?

Art viewing can be solitary, as reading often is. Even art viewing with an inquiry-based methodology can be solitary or conducted in small groups like book clubs. What are the benefits of engaging in full-class, inquiry-based discussion around works of art? These classroomwide discussions help students to better understand four things: First, they will better understand the work of art. Second, they will better understand the world, through vocabulary and knowledge building. Third, they will better understand each other. And finally, they will better understand what communal exploration and learning look like.

Understanding the Work of Art

Understanding a work of art involves considering multiple interpretations. Often art historians build on each other's interpretations, slowly building a bigger, richer, multifaceted understanding of a work of art. Students engaging in inquiry with art as a class can better understand a work of art through the multitude of perspectives they bring to the work of art and share with the groups.

As individuals, students each notice different elements of the work of art. One teacher told us, "A lot of my quietest kids actually spoke and said things . . . that even adults didn't. They noticed things in the artwork that even teachers didn't notice" (Randi Korn & Associates, 2007, p. 105). As different art historians attend to different aspects of an artwork, so students also attend to different aspects of an artwork, approaching it with different interests and experiences.

As a community, students put forth multiple interpretations of the work of art, some defensible and others not. As a community, they vet these ideas through examining the evidence for them. In the Art Investigation about Faith Ringgold's *Tar Beach* described earlier in this chapter, students work communally to determine what the children in the picture are sleeping on—is it a bed? a mattress? blankets? They share what they notice and their evidence for thinking one interpretation is more likely than another.

Students, like any community of learners, build on each other's ideas. When one student looking at Edgar Degas's *Dancers in Green and Yellow* considers that the dancers might be waiting nervously backstage, other students begin to notice aspects of the painting that evidence a backstage location or the nervousness of the dancers. One student takes this aspect of the discussion and wonders if this is why Degas created the piece—is he particularly interested in what it feels like to stand in the wings, waiting to perform?

As a community, these students have come to a more nuanced and careful understanding of the work of art than any single student might have. This is accomplished through communally sharing individual noticings, addressing questions, and responding to each other's ideas. At the same time, students are sharing their knowledge of the world and their vocabulary to describe the world. In this way, looking at art becomes an excellent opportunity to better understand the world.

Understanding the World

A critical challenge in the classroom is some students' lack of general knowledge about and vocabulary to describe the world. Numerous educators have noted that the more you know, the more easily you can learn new information (Caillies, Denhière, & Kintsch, 2002; Willingham, 2006). Studies have made it very clear that low-income students from homes with less educated families are less likely than other children to learn this type of information at home (Hirsch, 2006). For example, children from lower income homes generally have a smaller vocabulary than children of from higher income homes. The difference is dramatic: 3-year-olds with parents who are well-paid professionals have vocabularies of 1,100 words; children from low-income households have vocabularies of about 525 words (Tough, 2006). By first grade, the gap has grown: children from higher income households have vocabularies of about 20,000 words, while children from lower income households have vocabularies of about 5,000 words (California Department of Education, n.d.).

Students are often confronted with unfamiliar places, objects, and circumstances when they view a work of art. In the Art Investigation with *Dancers in Green and Yellow*, one student noticed "something that might be the background for the thing that they might dance to." The teacher used this as an opportunity to share a little about the theater: "It sounds like you're saying that this is part of the *stage set*. Do you all know that term? The things that come in and out, on and off the stage." Because this conversation is taking place with an entire class, a large group of students learn the term *stage set* and something about the world of theater.

In another classroom, students discussed *Composition 8*, an abstract painting by Vasily Kandinsky (Plate 4). After spending time observing the painting, the teacher asked the third-grade students, "If we were going to pick some words that this picture makes us think about, what words might we choose?" Student answers included the following list of words: *abstract, shapes, patterns, symbols, colors, imagination, symmetry, music, lines, geometry, fractions, money, circles, bouncing, white, blending, mixing, overlapping*. The teacher then shared some words that an art historian used to describe Kandinsky's painting, defining them for the students: "Calm, but dynamic. Aggressive and quiet. Pulsating" (Spector, 2009). The teacher asked students what they thought of these descriptive words. Student answers indicated that they understood these words.

"I would agree that it's pulsating, because the squiggly line looks like a beat."

"It looks dynamic, because all the shapes are going around everywhere."

A child who did not know the words *symmetry* or *geometry* or *pulsating* might learn them from this conversation. Collaboratively, the students are building their ability to describe the world. This language increases the students' abilities to communicate with others about shared human experience and broadens the knowledge base on which to build yet more knowledge.

Understanding Each Other

Building knowledge and vocabulary is a critical concern; it is one of the most important things that happens in the classroom. Beyond this knowledge base, inquiry-based conversations about art also help students better understand their classroom community. They learn what their classmates know and wonder, and they learn about the ideas held by different students. Because of the nature of personal meaning making, students often share information about their families and their lives. For example, while looking at *Tar Beach* students might discuss how they spend time with their families, or whether they live in an apartment with a roof like this. This knowledge helps students understand the experiences that have made their classmates who they are. Terry Barrett (2003) writes, "When a group of people interprets a work of art out loud . . . we have opportunities to learn about the object being interpreted, but we also have an opportunity to learn about the people who are giving their interpretations" (p. xvii).

While many other classroom discussions center around a few vocal students, in an Art Investigation even usually quiet students speak up. Children who do not volunteer to talk in other contexts find they have a great deal to share about a work of art. Students feel safe when they know there is no right answer and everyone is contributing to the building of ideas. In this context it is the students, rather than only the teacher, who are the experts. In this environment, students truly get to know even their quietest classmates.

Understanding where people come from helps students begin to understand the variety and validity of opinions. Students learn to tolerate different ideas and to understand why others think the way they do. They learn that it is acceptable to disagree with someone, but unacceptable not to listen or try to understand why they say what they do. These are essential skills for citizens of a democracy.

Understanding What Communal Exploration and Learning Look Like

Discussing art in a community in the context of an inquiry-based methodology helps students better understand what communal exploration and learning look like. There is tangible growth of understanding throughout the conversation. Questions are posed that can never be fully answered, but can be addressed as well as possible at that moment in time. In an Art Investigation it is clear that a single correct interpretation is impossible. It is also clear that careful looking and interpretation help make sense of what might initially seem incomprehensible, and that through large-group discussion of the artwork students can make enormous headway in beginning to understand the work for themselves. This is what it means to learn together.

THERE ARE MANY benefits of Art Investigations, from thinking and imagination skills to building general knowledge and understandings related to human communication. Art Investigations are also lessons students enjoy—a consideration that should not be ignored. The next two chapters, which focus on planning an Art Investigation and leading an Art Investigation in the classroom, offer teachers the tools to begin using this methodology with their students.

Chapter 2

PLANNING AN ART INVESTIGATION

IN THE CLASSROOM an Art Investigation can last anywhere from 10 minutes to over a half hour, depending on students' interest in the work and the time available for the discussion. Preparation for the Art Investigation does take some time. At first, it might take an hour or two to prepare; with experience and an archive of images, however, investigations can be planned much more quickly, perhaps in 10 or 15 minutes.

The steps in planning an Art Investigation are laid out in this chapter. They include selecting a subject area or theme, which can be related to almost any area of the curriculum, and a line of inquiry to explore (Steps 1 and 2); choosing a relevant image to discuss and briefly researching the artwork (Steps 3 and 4); and drafting open-ended, engaging questions to ask students with information incorporated where it will further the students' ability to interpret the work (Steps 5–7). Art Investigations always include the following:

1. An observation prompt at the beginning of the engagement with the work of art
2. Open-ended questions that encourage analysis and synthesis of new ideas, prior knowledge, and/or information about the artwork
3. Information related to the work of art or the artist that helps students think more deeply about the theme and the artwork, followed by questions that build on this information

Throughout the conversations, students should also be encouraged to make personal connections with the artwork and should be offered opportunities to engage with the art using different modalities.

I have imagined a hypothetical middle-school teacher to model each stage of planning through the development of a sample Art Investigation. Throughout this chapter this voice can be found in this typeface, in the sections delineated by rules.

STEP 1: CHOOSE A THEME

The first question you will grapple with in planning an Art Investigation is what kind of conversation you want to spark and whether, or how, to link this lesson with other areas of the curriculum. Will the Art Investigation help students better understand a culture or time period under consideration in a social studies unit? Will the Art Investigation be linked to an art lesson in composition? Is the class engaged in a study of how artists and poets use symbolism?

The Guggenheim encourages framing an Art Investigation around a single, targeted theme. One can revisit a work of art daily and see and think about new things; conversations about Marc Chagall's *Paris Through the Window* (Plate 2) in the Guggenheim Museum—with different groups, at different times—have explored the use of fantasy, the depiction of Paris, modernity, color, animals in art, the notion of a two-faced person and duality of personality, immigration, artistic composition, and more. However, during a 20-minute conversation with a classroom full of students, it is not possible to address all of these connections or themes in a meaningful way. It is best to choose a single theme or area of exploration related to a piece and allow time to explore it deeply.

Table 2.1 offers a chart of the artworks discussed by students in Chapter 1, and possible themes that might guide an Art Investigation.

I WANT TO LINK my inquiry to junior high science because that is what I teach. I'd like to focus on human biology, which my eighth-grade students are learning about. I'm choosing this area both because I'm interested in art about the human body—and there's a lot of it!—and because it's something I want my students to think more deeply and personally about.

STEP 2: IDENTIFY A LINE OF INQUIRY OR TARGETED AREA OF STUDENT UNDERSTANDING

Once you choose a theme for the Art Investigation, it is useful to think broadly about what related questions you want students to explore. Art Investigations work best when they are open-ended explorations that access the imagination, and this happens where there is space for students to consider their own ideas and opinions in the context of the subject. This type of exploration opens the door for students to learn more about their lived experience and their ideas about the world through the lens of the artwork. Through a dialogue related

Table 2.1. Works of Art and Possible Art Investigation Themes

Artwork	Theme from Chapter 1	Other possible themes for this artwork
Edgar Degas, *Dancers in Green and Yellow*	How artists and writers try to influence the world	The theatrical experience; body language
Faith Ringgold, *Tar Beach*	Urban community	Family; storytelling
Vasily Kandinsky, *Composition 8*	Interpreting abstraction	Movement; shape

to a big, open line of inquiry, art can take on a central role in students' examination of what matters to them. In other words, you will be identifying what Grant Wiggins and Jay McTighe (1998) call the "enduring understandings" of the unit. What is it that you want students to better understand after they participate in the Art Investigation?

When the investigation is too specific or factual, the line of inquiry ceases to be open-ended. For example, "What are the systems of the human body?" is a very limited line of inquiry; there is a correct set of answers to this question, with no room for inventiveness or personal interpretation. This is not an area of understanding, but rather a list to be memorized.

Big, open-ended lines of inquiry allow students to make personal meaning out of a work of art and generate a discussion that pushes student thinking to new places. An example of this type of inquiry or area of understanding as it relates to human biology might be: "What is the relationship between the 'true self' and the body?"—a question answered differently by different cultures and different eras.

Open-ended inquiries access and mirror the work that artists genuinely do: Artists respond to questions or themes that are of importance to them; they try to better understand or make sense of the world; and they use their imaginations to convey people, places, objects, ideas, or abstractions. For example, Edgar Degas painted dancers, and Pablo Picasso painted a woman ironing, in part in order to look at the otherwise invisible working-class world. Vasily Kandinsky painted abstractions to explore how art could help us free ourselves from the material world. These works are not exercises in composition, or replicas of people, places, or scenes; they are the result of people exploring big ideas and making sense of the world through visual expression.

Because at this point you have not yet chosen a work of art to look at with students, it is useful to think broadly about your unit and the various understandings that you want students to explore during an Art Investigation. Once you have chosen a work of art you can better match a line of inquiry to that work, and hone your ideas about what students should explore in this Art Investigation.

I REALLY WANT students to understand the interrelationship between their bodies and their minds and between their bodies and the world. For example, I want them to think about how good nutrition and sleep strengthen the body, and how the body needs oxygen and breathes out carbon dioxide for the trees—that we are small systems that are part of a larger system. I want them to question the things scientists and doctors know and think they know. For example, what is Ritalin? Why does it calm students down? What is it really doing, and why do so many students take it, and should they? In my science unit, some of the big questions are:

- How do the parts of the body relate to the whole?
- What does it mean to be healthy? How do we achieve this?
- What do we know about the human body, and what cultural or personal beliefs do we have that are unrelated to science? (For example, is the heart really the site of love, do we really only use a small portion of our brain, and will cold air really make you sick?) How do we distinguish fact from fiction?

STEP 3: SELECT AN ARTWORK

Once you have identified a theme and a possible line or lines of inquiry, the challenge is to find an artwork that will engage students in a consideration of that subject. This is not a linear process; it is a dialogue between the works that interest you and the questions and understandings essential to the subject area at hand.

As you begin to consider artworks to look at in your classroom, there are a few criteria to keep in mind. Clearly, the works of art selected—like texts chosen for read-aloud or independent reading—must be appropriate for your students. Aside from the work that would obviously not be permitted in schools due to nudity or violence, there are politically driven pieces that require an understanding of gender or race that a third-grade student will not have acquired, but a seventh-grade student may have or may be ready to begin considering. For example, Cindy Sherman's *Untitled Film Still* series (see Figure 2.1 for one of these photos) shows the artist in poses and settings that resemble film stills featuring different stereotypes of women. Middle school students can have a rich conversation about the mass media and stereotyping; second or third graders are probably not ready for this conversation. On the other hand, abstract or conceptual pieces that generally perplex adults who are novice art viewers often intrigue children, who have no difficulty accepting these works as art.

Just as important, the artwork needs to spark your interest. Enthusiasm is contagious, and will set the stage for a productive and interesting discussion. It is the rare occasion when a great conversation emerges in front of an artwork that does not engage the educator leading the discussion. Note that "engagement" or "interest" are not the same as "like"—an artwork that interests you might be one you have questions about, or are puzzled by, and want to spend time trying to better understand.

To find images, you might flip through art books or museum Web sites, conduct a Google image search, or visit a museum. Look for images that relate to your theme and line of inquiry. Find a few images to try working with, and start with the one that is the best match or the most appealing to you personally.

Figure 2.1. Cindy Sherman.
Untitled Film Still #15, 1978
Black-and-white photograph
sheet: 10 x 8 inches (25.4 x 20.3 cm);
image: 9 7/16 x 7 7/16, edition 2/10
Solomon R. Guggenheim Museum, New York
Purchased with funds contributed by the International Director's Council and Executive Committee Members Eli Broad, Elaine Terner Cooper, Ronnie Heyman, J. Tomilson Hill, Dakis Joannou, Barbara Lane, Robert Mnuchin, Peter Norton, Thomas Walther, and Ginny Williams 97.4573

Figure 2.2. Rineke Dijkstra.
Coney Island, N.Y., USA, July 9, 1993
(from the *Beaches* series), 1993
Chromogenic print
46 3/8 x 36 7/8 inches (117.8 x 93.7 cm),
edition 1/6
Solomon R. Guggenheim Museum, New York
Purchased with funds contributed by the
Harriett Ames Charitable Trust 2000.110

While looking for images, begin to create a file (electronic and/or paper) of images that interest you or that relate to other areas you teach. This file will make it much easier to prepare for future Art Investigations. It also challenges you to begin an ongoing relationship with art: Notice artworks at museums, in magazines, and on the Internet. What appeals to you? Print or photocopy it, or buy a postcard. Begin thinking about what art you like and why.

I'm JUST GOING to look at the Guggenheim Museum's Web site for art for now, since I don't have much time, and I could easily spend hours searching the Internet for an image. I'm familiar with a few of the artists, but will also just experiment by clicking on the names of different artists.

After spending a while searching (time flew!), I found a few images that are very clearly related to biology:

- Kiki Smith, *Ribs* (Plate 5)—this seems to be an artist's interpretation of a body part (ribs).
- Rineke Dijkstra, *Coney Island* series (see Figure 2.2)—these are images of children, who are about the same age as my students.

- Ann Hamilton's *Untitled* series—these are videos of body parts (mouth, ear, and so on) in odd situations: a mouth full of rocks (see Figure 2.3), a neck with water pouring down it.
- I think I'll start by trying to work with Kiki Smith's *Ribs*, because I think my students will be intrigued by it, and because it's my favorite of these three options. This piece might work with my question, "What do we know about the human body, and what cultural or personal beliefs do we have that are unrelated to science? How do we distinguish fact from fiction?"

STEP 4: RESEARCH THE ARTWORK
AND CONFIRM THE LINE OF INQUIRY

It is difficult, if not impossible, to teach something without having learned about it yourself. To lead an Art Investigation, you do not need to have a degree in art history, or read art books in your free time, or have conducted general research into art. You do need to know a little bit about the image you show to students and about the artist who created it.

The best way to get to know a work of art is to spend time looking at it. What do you notice? What do you like about the artwork? What interests you? What questions do you have? How might it relate to your theme or possible lines of inquiry? Become familiar with the artwork; think of this as a conversation such as you might have with a guest speaker before bringing him or her into the classroom. Looking at a work of art with a friend or colleague and having an informal conversation about the work is also a great way to get to know the piece. If you do this before you read about it, you will find that often much of what is written about a work of art are descriptions of details that you can notice on your own.

That said, it is a good idea to read a few paragraphs about the artist and the work of art as background. This will provide you with some basic information about the piece, as well as making more evident what areas remain unknown or unclear to you (which it is always OK to admit to students). Content knowledge builds quickly: After spending a year bringing art into the classroom, you will find you have a surprisingly good knowledge base about art on which to build.

After researching your artwork, take a few minutes to confirm your line of inquiry. In doing this, you are also confirming your goals regarding the understandings students will gain from engaging in this Art Investigation. It is important to clarify this for yourself before writing specific questions you

Figure 2.3. Ann Hamilton. *untitled (the capacity of absorption),* 1988/93
Color-toned video on LCD screen, silent, 30 min.
3 1/2 x 4 1/2 inches (8.9 x 11.4 cm), edition 3/9
Solomon R. Guggenheim Museum, New York
Gift, The Peter Norton Family Foundation 94.4260

will ask; with Art Investigations, as with all teaching, goals for student learning drive the lesson.

LOOKING AT Kiki Smith's *Ribs,* I am noting the fragility, and the way in which this
piece is both similar to and different from real ribs. It's very fragmented. And why
is it pink? I think of bones as off-white, but the vaguely pink color is somehow
very biological—it rings true. It's also somewhat feminine—maybe because of
both the color and the fragility I assume that these are female ribs. Some pieces
are completely detached, and I wonder how they store the work and reinstall it
each time—does it always look the same? And are you supposed to be able to
see the strings?

Now that I have looked at the piece for a while, I read the short essays on the
artwork and on the artist that I printed from the Guggenheim Museum's *Collection Online,* written by Jennifer Blessing (2009). The piece is from 1987; during
the 1980s a number of artists were interested in the human body. Kiki Smith often
focuses on the body: "fragmented and whole, depicted relatively realistically yet

always suggestively altered." She is interested in body and identity, and body and emotion, not direct representation. In 1979 Smith looked at Gray's *Anatomy of the Human Body* as a source for drawings about the human body. Then she made sculptures of the human circulatory system, nervous system, skin, and organs. *Ribs* is terra-cotta; the parts of the rib cage are strung together and held up like a marionette suspended from the wall. Pink rib bones, disconnected from the sternum, show repaired breaks—evidence of trauma? Fragile. The display is like a specimen at a natural history museum. Also of interest (from Smith's bio): in 1985, propelled by an interest in obtaining practical knowledge about the body, Smith studied to become an emergency medical technician.

I spent a few minutes looking online for Smith's other related work, but was only able to find images of one. When I have more time I'd like to go to the library and look up these other pieces.

When I look back at the possibilities of inquiry that I listed earlier, I see that this artwork lends itself to talking about what we know versus what we believe about the human body: fact versus fiction, biology versus symbolism. I want students to understand that artists research the biology of the body, but also have their own ideas about the body and its symbolism. I want students to understand that each of us has both knowledge of the body itself and also ideas about fragility, love, self, endurance, and so on that are cultural and personal beliefs related to the body. I want students to understand that these beliefs are valid and important, but that that they are not the same as an understanding of human biology.

STEP 5: WRITE AN OBSERVATION QUESTION

The educator and philosopher Maxine Greene (2001) writes about how the richness and depth of our interpretations of a work of art "may well be a function of the intensity of our attending" (p. 11). This "attending," or careful observation, is critical to understanding a work of art. Students should be encouraged to spend time looking at an image and articulating what they see before they begin to contemplate what they think it means. It can be argued that even the most basic observations are a form of interpretation; by choosing what to focus on, or giving words to what is happening in a scene, or describing a shape by noting what it reminds you of, you are engaging in the work of interpretation. That said, when students (or any viewers of art) jump to larger interpretive ideas—why Kiki Smith might have created a sculpture of ribs or why the cat in *Paris Through the Window* has a human face—without first fully attending to what they see, they often make assumptions based on misunderstandings or misperceptions.

The first question when looking at a work of art should focus the students on careful observation. An appropriate question might be "What do you see?" or "What do you notice?" Other observation strategies and prompts include the following:

- Ask students to spend some time looking at the artwork before any discussion of it. Don't allow any students to raise their hands or speak during this period.
- Have students share what they notice with a partner (often called "turn and talk" or "pair share"). In this way, everyone gets a chance to talk. Once students have a few minutes to share in pairs, some or all of these pairs might share something interesting they observed with the larger group.
- Challenge students to make a list, either alone or in pairs, of at least 10–15 things they notice in the painting. Make sure their lists are long, because the first five or so will be the obvious ones; after they have listed these they will begin noticing more interesting details.
- Ask students to sketch the artwork. Be sure to remind them to look as carefully as possible, and tell them that this exercise is about careful looking, not making something beautiful. You can let them know that sketching is a tool artists use to observe the world, as well as works of art, more carefully.

It is critical to root interpretations in observation, and an initial observation question helps students do this. Additionally, beginning an Art Investigation with a general observation question allows students to notice and consider what about the artwork interests them. For example, if looking at Kiki Smith's *Ribs,* students might be interested in the strings that seem to both hold the work up and dangle from individual ribs, or in the insectlike shape of the piece. Letting them explore their observations in an open way allows the piece to become interesting and meaningful to them in ways that cannot possibly be predicted, and helps them interpret the work later in the process.

I WANT STUDENTS to look for a while before they begin talking; otherwise I'll hear from the same 3 or 4 kids who always talk. I'm hopeful that in this way new voices will emerge. My observation prompt will be: "Take a look at the artwork represented here. (Allow for at least one full minute of silent looking.) What do you notice?"

STEP 6: BRAINSTORM, SELECT,
AND SEQUENCE INTERPRETIVE QUESTIONS

In the Art Investigation about Edgar Degas's *Dancers in Green and Yellow* that was introduced in Chapter 1, after asking an observation question, the teacher asks the following two questions:

- "What do you think is interesting to Degas about these dancers backstage?"
- "What are some ideas you have for how Degas might have wanted to change how people thought?"

These questions ask students to infer the artist's intent and interest. The latter question challenges students to synthesize their understanding of the artwork with prior knowledge, in this case their previous explorations of how artists challenge people to think in new ways. This question also brings students around to an explicit investigation of the intended line of inquiry: how artists try to influence people's ideas about the world.

Both questions are open ended. An open-ended question is one that has many, many correct answers. It must be broad enough for students to access and share their own opinions, and open enough to allow for multiple, conflicting correct answers. Open-ended interpretive questions tend to access the "how," "why," or "what if," rather than the "what" of a painting.

Considering artist's intent is a question that art critics and art historians regularly engage in. It is open-ended in that an artist's true intent can never be completely confirmed, often not even by artists themselves. In order to allow for the fact that all statements about artist's intent are hypotheses, art historians use the conditional. In the essay about Marc Chagall's *Paris Through the Window* on the Guggenheim's Web site, curator Jennifer Blessing (2009) writes: "[The Eiffel Tower] served as a metaphor for Paris and perhaps modernity itself. Chagall's parachutist might also refer to contemporary experience, since the first successful jump occurred in 1912. Other motifs suggest the artist's native Vitebesk [a town in Russia]." Note the words *perhaps, might,* and *suggest.* The author does not know for certain what Marc Chagall was thinking when he painted this, but her job as an art historian and curator is to try to make sense of the artist's choices. Likewise, given time to look and think, students can make excellent guesses about what an artist might have intended. It is important, however, to pose questions in the conditional tense—for example, "How do you think Degas *might* have wanted to change how people

Table 2.2. Sample of Lines of Inquiry in Three Art Investigations

Artwork	Theme	Closed-ended line of inquiry	Open-ended line of inquiry
Edgar Degas, *Dancers in Green and Yellow*	Gesture	What are these dancers doing? How do these poses show us what they are doing?	Take the pose of one of the dancers. What might she be thinking? How can pose or gesture convey something about character?
Faith Ringgold *Tar Beach*	Detail in writing	What part of the story does this artwork show us? What details are in the artwork that are not in the text?	Pick a detail that is of interest to you. What does this detail tell us about the place and people? If you were going to make changes to this artwork, how else might you share this information?
Vassily Kandinsky, *Composition 8*	Geometry/ Shape	What shapes are in this painting?	Create a composition using at least three different types of triangles. Then compare your composition to Kandinsky's *Composition 8*. How are they similar or different? What are some things you notice about his use of triangles?

thought?"—rather than the unconditional—"How *did* Degas want to change how people thought?" Careful use of language can ensure that you are asking students for their ideas about what an artist could have been thinking, rather than uncovering the unarguable "truth."

Table 2.2 shows a few examples of closed-ended and open-ended questions for works we have already looked at.

In writing interpretive questions, it is helpful to follow a three-step procedure:

1. List as many questions as possible that are open-ended and might support exploration of this line of inquiry.
2. Select the two to four questions that best guide students from open-ended observation through analysis related to this line of inquiry.
3. Sequence these questions.

MY LINE OF inquiry that relates to this Art Investigation is: "What do we know about the human body, and what cultural or personal beliefs do we have that are unrelated to science? How do we distinguish fact from fiction?"

I want students to understand that artists research the biology of the body, but also have their own ideas about symbolism; that each of us has both knowledge of the body itself and also ideas about fragility, love, self, endurance, and so on that are cultural and personal beliefs related to the body; that these beliefs are valid and important, but that that they are not the same as an understanding of human biology.

Questions that might help students analyze the artwork in light of this line of inquiry and these goals . . . hmmm . . .

A few initial ideas:

- What does this artwork make you think about?
- What about ribs might have interested the artist?
- How is this sculpture similar to or different from real human ribs?
- What choices did the artist make about how to depict ribs?
- What might the artist think about the human body that is derived from cultural beliefs rather than biological information?
- How might this artwork be different if it were displayed in a different way?
- What do you think/know about or associate with ribs/bones?
- How are the artist's ideas different from yours?

Looking over my ideas, some questions are better for this particular Art Investigation than others:

- "What does this artwork make you think about?" I wonder if this question is too broad for my students.
- "What about ribs might have interested the artist?" I like this question; very in line with my theme.
- "How is this sculpture similar to or different from real human ribs?" If I ask this question, it would be early on in the Art Investigation. It's not so open, but perhaps could be a nice way to move from observation into interpretation.
- "What choices did the artist make about how to depict ribs?" Very similar to the question above. I wonder if my students would find this question hard to answer.

- "What might the artist think about the human body that is derived from cultural beliefs rather than biological information?" Definitely too complicated a question.
- "How might this artwork be different if it were displayed in a different way?" I like this question, but not really on track for my theme.
- "What do you think/know about or associate with ribs / bones?" I think I have to ask this at some point. Maybe before they talk about what the artist might think, they could share what they think.
- "How are the artist's ideas different from yours?" This is the clear comparison if I ask about their ideas about ribs/bones and then about the artist's. I wonder if there is a way to get them to articulate—or even sketch—symbolic or fictional ideas about the ribs or the body that they have?

OK, so maybe my best questions are these:

- "How is this sculpture similar to or different from human ribs? What are some of the choices the artist is making?"
- "Why might the artist have made some of these choices?"
- "What do you know—associate with—value—about bones or ribs?"

STEP 7: IDENTIFY INFORMATION THAT WILL FURTHER THE CONVERSATION

Information is one of the tools that can help push students' thinking further when used well (but prevent individual thought when misused). When information relevant to the general focus of the investigation is offered in small amounts and at appropriate times, it offers students new opportunities to make connections and reconsider ideas.

There is some difference of opinion in the museum education world about how much information to provide about a work of art. Adults crave information, yet without the opportunity to actively think about this information they may forget much of what they hear (Willingham, 2003). Students are also likely to forget information when they are not challenged to think about it, or when they are not given the opportunity to form associations between new and prior knowledge.

Given the right conditions—time, attention, personal interest—one can certainly look at an artwork, make some sense of it, and react to it, without any outside information. If the goal is to make a personal connection to a work of art, information may not be necessary; in fact, it might inhibit a genuine response. The goal of Art Investigations, however, is to help students understand or make meaning from a work of art, and to teach them how to learn from and about a work of art they might encounter on their own. Often Art Investigations have the added goal of helping students develop an understanding of specific people, times, places, or ideas. In an Art Investigation, information helps the learner make new connections and inspires new ideas and understandings about a work of art.

Information helps people make sense of the world. It is important, however, to be very selective about the information you offer during an Art Investigation. What students will take away from an Art Investigation are the ideas that result from the interactions of new ideas and the action of thought. Therefore, the information offered during an inquiry-based discussion should be carefully chosen, related to well-crafted follow-up questions, and shared with students at the most relevant point in the conversation, never before students have had a chance to observe the artwork in depth.

The information to be shared might be as basic as the name of a painting, or the time and place in which it was painted. A child looking at *Paris Through the Window* may not recognize Paris or the Eiffel Tower, and—in the context of a lesson on landmarks—sharing with students that this is Paris, and that the tall structure is the Eiffel Tower, might spark new thoughts on the importance of landmarks both abroad and at home. In different discussions about the same painting, it might become important to share that Chagall was Russian and was living in Paris at the time he painted this, or that this work was painted in 1913 and that the Eiffel Tower and parachutist may be symbols of modernity. The information presented will depend on the theme of the Art Investigation and what information will help students delve deeper into the relationship of the artwork to that theme. It is unlikely that more than one of these chunks of information would be relevant to a 20-minute Art Investigation.

What information you feel best moves the conversation forward should be followed by a question that allows the students to synthesize this information with their own ideas, as well as with what they see in the work of art. The goal of information is not to end the conversation with an answer, but to spark new ideas and associations. In the case of *Paris Through the Window*, after telling students that this is Paris and that the tall structure is the Eiffel Tower, a teacher might say, "Let's think of as many reasons as we can why the artist might have included this landmark in his painting."

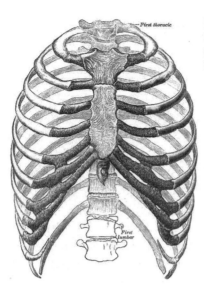

Figure 2.4. The thorax from in front.
From Henry Gray, *Anatomy of the Human Body*
(Philadelphia: Lea & Febiger,1918). Available at
http://www.bartleby.com/107/

Alternately, the information about symbols of modernity might be followed by the question, "How do these symbols of modernity fit in with the rest of the painting?"

SINCE MUCH OF the conversation will focus on Kiki Smith's and the students' interpretations of ribs, I'd like to share that she was looking at a picture of ribs from a biology book as inspiration for this piece, that it is rooted in actual biological information. I could even show them a picture of ribs from Gray's *Anatomy of the Human Body* (Figure 2.4), so we could compare them—that would provide a very memorable look at an important part of the skeletal structure.

The steps in planning an Art Investigation discussed in this chapter have been modeled through the development of an Art Investigation plan focusing on Kiki Smith's *Ribs,* exploring how artists interpret the human body. In order to plan this Art Investigation, our hypothetical teacher has done the following work:

- Identified the subject area and line of inquiry that the Art Investigation will target
- Identified and researched an artwork, and then confirmed the line of inquiry along with goals for student understanding
- Written and sequenced observation and interpretation questions
- Inserted a little relevant information

This work has resulted in a plan ready to be taken into the classroom. The final Art Investigation plan, edited by mulling over it a few times, is as follows:

- Take a look at the artwork represented here. (Allow for at least one full minute of silent looking.) What do you notice?
- This picture is from Henry Gray's *Anatomy of the Human Body*, an anatomy book that the artist, Kiki Smith, looked at as a model for *Ribs*. In what ways is her sculpture similar to or different from this sketch of human ribs?
- The artist who created the illustration of the ribs in *Gray's Anatomy* was trying to create the clearest, most accurate image as a resource for doctors. Kiki Smith had a different goal and made different choices. Why might Kiki Smith have chosen to depict ribs, and why might she have made the choices she did?
- Take a minute and sketch an idea for your own artwork that uses some part of the human body to convey a message or idea about human existence.
- Compare your ideas to Kiki Smith's. Do you have any new thoughts on *Ribs*?

Once an Art Investigation plan is written, it is helpful to take the time to try it out on a friend or colleague. These discussions often lead to small changes that make for a more successful lesson in the classroom. After that is done, the plan is ready to present in the classroom. The next chapter contains advice on how to work with this plan to lead a lively and open, rather than scripted, conversation.

Plate 1. Edgar Degas. *Dancers in Green and Yellow (Danseuses vertes et jaunes)*, ca. 1903
Pastel on several pieces of paper, mounted on board
38 7/8 x 28 1/8 inches (98.8 x 71.5 cm)
Solomon R. Guggenheim Museum, New York
Thannhauser Collection, Gift, Justin K. Thannhauser, 78.2514.12

Plate 2. Mark Chagall. *Paris Through the Window (Paris par la fenêtre)*, 1913
Oil on canvas
53 1/2 x 55 3/4 inches (135.8 x 141.4 cm)
Solomon R. Guggenheim Museum, New York
Solomon R. Guggenheim Founding Collection, by gift 37.438

Plate 3. Faith Ringgold. *Tar Beach (Part I of the Woman on a Bridge series)*, 1988
Acrylic on canvas, bordered with printed, painted, quilted, and pieced cloth
74 5/8 x 68 1/2 inches (189.5 x 174 cm)
Solomon R. Guggenheim Museum, New York
Gift, Mr. and Mrs. Gus and Judith Lieber 88.3620
Faith Ringgold © 1988

Plate 4. Vasily Kandinsky. *Composition 8 (Komposition 8)*, July 1923
Oil on canvas
55 1/8 x 79 1/8 inches (140 x 201 cm)
Solomon R. Guggenheim Museum, New York
Solomon R. Guggenheim Founding Collection, by gift 37.262

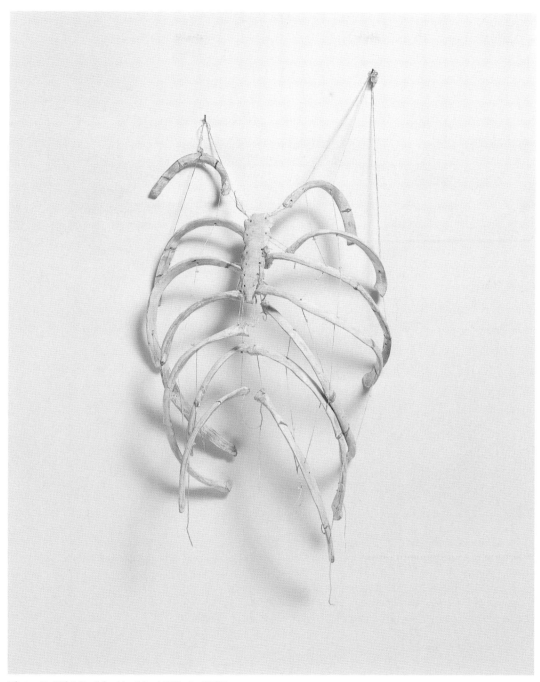

Plate 5. Kiki Smith. Untitled (*Ribs*), *1987*
Terracotta, ink, and thread
20 x 15 x 9 inches (50.8 x 38.1 x 22.9 cm)
© Kiki Smith, courtesy Pace Wildenstein, New York
Solomon R. Guggenheim Museum, New York
Purchased with funds contributed by The Peter Norton Family Foundation 93.4241

Plate 6. Vincent van Gogh. *Mountains at Saint-Rémy (Montagnes à Saint-Rémy),* July 1889
Oil on canvas
28 1/4 x 35 3/4 inches (71.8 x 90.8 cm)
Solomon R. Guggenheim Museum, New York
Thannhauser Collection, Gift, Justin K. Thannhauser 78.2514.24

Plate 7. Mark Chagall.
*Green Violinist
(Violiniste)*, 1923–24
Oil on canvas
78 x 42 3/4 inches
(198 x 108.6 cm)
Solomon R. Guggenheim
Museum, New York
Solomon R. Guggenheim
Founding Collection,
by gift 37.446

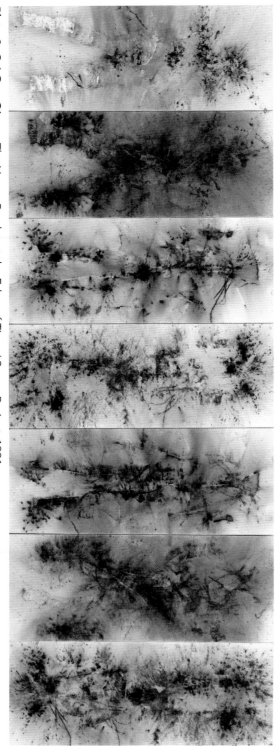

Plate 8. Cai Guo-Qiang. *The Vague Border at the Edge of Time / Space Project,* 1991
Gunpowder on paper, mounted on wood as seven panel folding screen 78 3/4 × 234 1/4 (200 × 595 cm)
Collection Fondation Cartier pour l'art contemporain, Paris

Plate 9. Vasily Kandinsky. *Blue Mountain (Der blaue Berg)*, 1908–09
Oil on canvas
41 3/4 x 38 inches (106 x 96.6 cm)
Solomon R. Guggenheim Museum, New York
Solomon R. Guggenheim Founding Collection, by gift 41.505

Plate 10. Arshile Gorky. *Untitled*, summer 1944
Oil on canvas
65 3/4 x 70 3/16 inches (167 x 178.2 cm)
The Solomon R. Guggenheim Foundation
Peggy Guggenheim Collection, Venice 76.2553.152

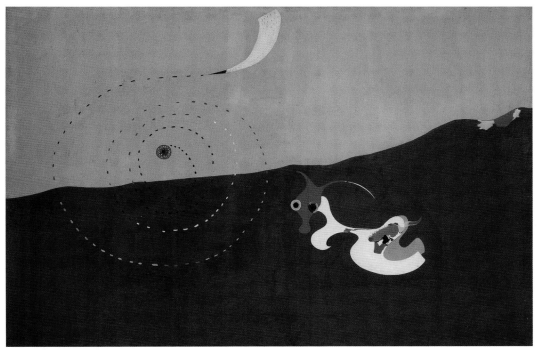

Plate 11. Joan Miró. *Landscape (The Hare) (Paysage [Le Lièvre])*, autumn 1927
Oil on canvas
51 x 76 5/8 inches (129.6 x 194.6 cm)
Solomon R. Guggenheim Museum, New York 57.1459

Plate 12. Rufino Tamayo. *Heavenly Bodies,* 1946
Oil with sand on canvas
34 x 41 3/8 inches (86.3 x 105 cm)
The Solomon R. Guggenheim Foundation
Peggy Guggenheim Collection, Venice 76.2553.119

Plate 13. Andrea Zittel. *A-Z Wagon Station customized by Russell Whitten*, 2003 (closed view)
Powder-coated steel, medium-density fiberboard (MDF), aluminum, Lexan, two velvet pads, dirt-bike jersey and pants, helmet, boots, gloves, three gears, photographs, and lip balm
61 x 82 x 57 inches (154.9 x 208.3 x 144.8 cm)
Solomon R. Guggenheim Museum, New York
Purchased with funds contributed by the Young Collectors Council and Geoffrey Fontaigne 2007.40

Plate 14. Camille Pissarro. *The Hermitage at Pontoise (Les Côteaux de l'Hermitage)*, ca. 1867
Oil on canvas
59 5/8 x 79 inches (151.4 x 200.6 cm)
Solomon R. Guggenheim Museum, New York
Thannhauser Collection, Gift, Justin K. Thannhauser 78.2514.67

Plate 15. Louise Bourgeois. *Maman,* 1999, cast 2001
Bronze, stainless steel, and marble
29 feet 4 3/8 inches x 32 feet 1 7/8 inches x 38 feet 5/8 inches (9 x 9.8 x 1.2 m), edition 2/6
Guggenheim Bilbao Museoa GBM2001.1

Plate 16. Jamie Wefald. *Untitled*, 2007
Acrylic on paper

Chapter 3

LEADING AN ART INVESTIGATION

AT THEIR BEST, Art Investigations are wandering, surprising conversations, in which teachers notice and learn as many new things about an artwork as the students do. They are also opportunities to get to know each other better: As students share what they notice and are interested in, make connections to their lives and other points of reference, and debate with each other about interpretation, they share valuable information with each other about who they are and what they care about. Art Investigations can foster a sense of community in the classroom, in which the group works together to create a shared understanding of a work of art while valuing individual interpretations and different ideas.

A few facilitation techniques are critical to ensuring the richness of these conversations. These tactics include using wait time, allowing for multiple answers, transitioning smoothly between questions, asking for evidence, responding to incorrect statements, and attending to student questions. Each of these is addressed in turn below, and then shown in use in the three Art Investigations that close the chapter.

FACILITATION TECHNIQUES

Using Wait Time

It sounds like common sense: After asking a question, wait for an answer—or even a few answers. But it is difficult to stand in front of a classroom, allowing for silence, hoping that the students are thinking about the question rather than daydreaming or waiting for you to say something else. In fact, studies have shown that, at least in science classrooms, teachers usually wait less than one second before they rephrase their question or answer the question themselves (Tobin, 1987).

To encourage students to think, and to provide them with the time to have sophisticated thoughts about complicated subjects, waiting at least 3 to

5 seconds for student answers is essential. This applies both after the teacher asks the question and after a student speaks, and the technique is called *wait time*. Numerous studies have proven that wait time leads to more student responses, more hypothesizing (indicating a willingness to take risks in sharing ideas), greater support of these hypotheses with evidence, more students responding to other students' ideas, and more responses from students whom teachers think of as "slow learners" (Tobin, 1987).

Educator and author Laurel Schmidt (2004) suggests that teachers train themselves to use wait time by "pretending to smoke"—acting as if you have all the time in the world, while allowing students to formulate their ideas:

> Lean against the chalkboard, assume the most nonchalant pose you can muster, and *visualize* smoking. Not the guilty little nips of people who swear they're trying to quit. I mean those long, pensive, lung-inflating drags that dyed-in-the-wool tobacco lovers take. . . . Smoke like that while you're waiting, and it will send a message to your students that you have all the time in the world. You're just going to hang out contentedly until they're ready to talk because your only interest is hearing what they *think*. (pp. 103–104)

In an Art Investigation, after posing a question, wait for students to answer. After one student answers, continue to wait, and allow other students to answer. Enjoy letting the students do most of the work.

Allowing for Multiple Answers

A corollary to wait time is listening to what students have to say—not one student, but as many students as possible. Allowing many students to share their responses to each question underscores that you are not looking for a single correct answer (which the first student to answer gave). Rather, you are asking a truly open-ended question and value a diversity of responses.

When the teacher responds after the first student answers, the conversation feels very teacher-directed. As observers or participants, we begin wondering about the teacher's agenda: what is she looking for? What does she want me to say? Allowing for multiple answers is synonymous with allowing for room for new ideas, and room for responses to new ideas. The conversation starts to belong to the students rather than the teacher.

Especially in the beginning of an Art Investigation—during the observational phase—take the time to allow at least three student answers before asking even a follow-up question (such as "What are you noticing that makes you say that?" or "Can you show us where you see that in the art work?"). This allows the conversation to begin flowing and creates an atmosphere of shared excitement about the work of art, as well as giving ownership of the conversation to the students.

True listening (as opposed to just letting students share their answers) is hard. It is challenging to listen for the unexpected, while keeping in mind the next step in your lesson. But by listening carefully to what the students really say, you learn more about the students, how they think, and what they have already learned in your classroom. And more often then not, students themselves provide answers that help lead you to the next question planned in the conversation—or somewhere unexpected but even better.

Transitioning Smoothly to the Next Question

After students have spent ample time (or as much time as you are able to allow during that particular lesson) addressing a question, you will want to ask your next question. If you simply stop and ask the next question, the conversation is halted, and the questions seem unrelated to each other. One technique for encouraging a flow of question and answer that feels more conversational is to introduce the next question by summarizing some of what you have already heard and using those statements to contextualize the next question.

In an Art Investigation with Vincent van Gogh's painting *Mountains at Saint-Rémy* (Plate 6), students spent time describing what they noticed in the painting; the teacher then wanted to ask them how they would feel if they could step inside the painting. She began this second question by noting some of what they had already commented on: "You've just described a lot of what's in this scene: the mountain, and the path, and the house and garden. You've also mentioned these dark lines and wavy brush strokes; one student said it made him feel sea sick! Let's think for a minute about how it would feel to step inside this painting, at any place in the painting you want to visit. What would you smell, or hear, or feel inside this painting?"

There are other techniques that can be used to make this transition smooth. You might phrase a question as though it comes out of the conversation: "As you describe this scene, I'm wondering what it would feel like to actually visit this place. What would you smell, or hear, or feel if you could step inside this painting?" Smooth transitions, whatever the technique used to make these transitions, encourage an ongoing conversation that builds from one question to the next, rather than stopping and starting again with each new question.

Asking for Evidence

When students begin to interpret an artwork in front of them, it shows that they are thinking critically. Students who are new to Art Investigations often share hypotheses without explaining where their ideas came from. Asking for evidence for these assertions—where in the work of art they see something that leads them to this idea—is essential to helping students understand the relationship between hypotheses and evidence. As discussed in Chapter 1, critical thinking involves understanding how one knows things, so asking for evidence challenges students to exercise those critical thinking muscles. Asking for evidence also facilitates debate, which leads to the assessment of ideas and the search for a more insightful answer or answers. When two students with differing ideas or interpretations both share their evidence for these assertions, the group goes deeper into the reading of the artwork. In this way students begin to understand that while all ideas are worth listening to, some ideas are more precise or insightful than others, because there is more evidence to back them up.

Asking for evidence also keeps the conversation focused on the work of art, which is the group's shared point of reference. It keeps the conversation rooted in the concrete and the communal, assuring that students can follow each other's line of thought. It makes evident passages in the artwork that might otherwise go unnoticed or unexamined. And it mirrors the process of curators, art historians, and art critics, who consistently refer back to the work of art in front of them.

When asking for evidence, follow up a student's answer with a question such as, "What do you see in the artwork that makes you say that?" or "What are you noticing that makes you think that?" If students are having trouble giving evidence, you might dedicate an Art Investigation to the practice of giving evidence, by explicitly asking for hypotheses about something (e.g., the mood of a painting or what the materials in an installation might symbolize) and creating a graphic organizer, such as a T-chart, listing both students' hypotheses and evidence.

Addressing Incorrect Statements

Even the most open-ended of questions can elicit incorrect answers. For example, Guggenheim educators have heard students conclude that Vincent van Gogh's *Mountains at Saint Rémy* is a picture of a garbage dump and that the udder of Franz Marc's *Yellow Cow* is a hand (see Figure 3.1). It is important not to let students leave the conversation with these misunderstandings.

Figure 3.1. Franz Marc. *Yellow Cow (Gelbe Kuh)*, 1911
Oil on canvas
55 3/8 x 74 1/2 inches (140.5 x 189.2 cm)
Solomon R. Guggenheim Museum, New York
Solomon R. Guggenheim Founding Collection 49.1210

To directly contradict the student, however, would interfere with the open nature of the conversation. How, then, does one address incorrect statements?

One way to address an incorrect statement is to pose a follow-up question that asks the student to share what he or she is noticing in the artwork that led to this statement. These questions are the same as those that ask for evidence and their purpose is similar: to ensure that students link hypotheses with evidence, which is one way to check the validity of an interpretation. A conversation in which a teacher asks a follow-up question to counter a misinformed response about the van Gogh painting might go like this:

A student says, "I think he's painting the place where they leave the garbage."

"Do you mean a garbage dump?" asks the teacher, to ensure that there is no misunderstanding of the student's statement. The student nods assent.

The teacher looks closely at the painting and then asks, "What are you noticing that makes you think this a garbage dump?"

"See all that brown, that's the garbage, in the dirt."

"So you're noticing that the color of some of these hills is brown, which makes you think it's dirt, not trees or grass, is that right?" Again, the student nods assent.

"What else are all of you noticing?"

Through this exchange, the teacher has reshaped the student's statement to be about what the student saw—the artist's use of the color brown, a color often associated with barren land—rather than the student's incorrect interpretation of these observations. Later, another student will hypothesize that this is a mountain and give evidence for this. At that point the teacher can say, "Great, so now we know that this is a mountain," to ensure that students do not leave the conversation thinking that this is a painting of a garbage dump. In this way, the teacher both affirms student contributions and ensures that the students do not blatantly misunderstand the painting.

A second way to counter incorrect answers is through sharing a small piece of relevant information. Often this is just the title or the year of the painting, or a tiny bit of information about the subject. Using this type of response to the same misinformation about van Gogh's painting, the teacher would have first clarified the student's comment and then responded, "Interesting. I can see why you might look at these brown shapes and think they are a garbage dump. I did a little research on this painting before showing it to you today, and one of the things I found out is that the title of the painting is *Mountains at Saint-Rémy* and that these are mountains in France. So now we know that these are mountains. Let's see if that information sparks any interesting observations."

Yet another strategy for addressing incorrect statements is to ask other students to respond, which invites students to help each other better understand the artwork. This strategy should be used carefully, discouraging students from disparaging each other's ideas. In the case of *Mountains at Saint-Rémy*, it would be better to ask students what kind of place they thought this might be, rather than whether they agree or disagree that this is a garbage dump. Using this strategy, the teacher might say, "I can see why you think that. Who else has an idea about what kind of place this could be?"

A word about using information to avoid misunderstandings about the work. The misunderstandings that should be corrected are basic mistakes, often stemming from children's lack of knowledge of the wider world. For example, the student who thought that *Mountains at Saint-Rémy* depicted a garbage dump might never have been hiking in the mountains. Likewise, a student from a town with stand-alone houses with slanted roofs might not understand where the family in *Tar Beach* (Plate 3) is, or what relationship that has to a roof. That said, it is important to leave room for students to make their own meaning from a work of art. When students view Marc Chagall's

Green Violinist (Plate 7), they sometimes make associations with Halloween or with Pete Seger's giant, Abiyoyo. In doing this, they are creating important understandings for themselves, connecting the green face to a mask, or the large man to giants from literature. While students might eventually want to know that Chagall was not from a community that celebrated Halloween, or that the story of Abiyoyo was written after *Green Violinist* was painted, these associations help students make meaning from the work (and evidence the meanings they are making) and should be valued for that reason.

Generally, one or a combination of these three methods—refocusing on observation by asking, "What are you seeing in the artwork that makes you say that?"; correcting an off-track assumption with some basic information about the piece, such as the title; or inviting other students to consider an aspect of the artwork that might be misunderstood—works to respond to an incorrect statement. These strategies should be combined with a general sensitivity to the goals of the conversation and the ways in which students interact with each other.

Addressing Student Questions

There are many reasons to encourage and value student questions. Addressing student questions is a way of explicitly valuing their contributions to the discussion. Questions are a sign of curiosity, of engagement with the material and with the world in general. Questions are a way for students to take responsibility for and control of their own learning, both in the classroom and beyond. Question posing is also a great strategy for understanding complex material, a process that students can use to understand what they see or read (Rosenshine, Meister, & Chapman, 1996).

Student questions are often requests for more information. Looking at *Mountains at Saint-Rémy,* a student might ask, "Who painted this?" or "Is that mountain near here?" If a teacher knows the answer to a student's factual question, there is no reason not to share it. The questions themselves contextualize the information, and the answers help students construct meaningful interpretations of the work of art. This is also a good way to build general knowledge about art and about the world.

When student questions are matters of opinion—for example, "Is this a good work of art?"—then ways to address this question include turning it back to the class, or sharing the opinions of others while carefully underscoring that these are opinions. Opinions might be followed up by asking students whether they agree or disagree.

In the first case, the conversation might look like this:

A student looking at *Mountains of Saint-Rémy* asks, "Is this a good painting?"

The teacher says, "That's an interesting question. 'Good' means different things to different people, and there are lots of works of art that people disagree about. What do all of you think?"

Alternately, the teacher might respond by sharing a general art world opinion, saying, "Hmmm. Well, a lot of art critics and art historians think so. Vincent van Gogh, who painted this, is a really famous artist, and he has a whole museum dedicated to his art in the Netherlands. But art is really subjective; some people might like an artwork that others dislike." In either case, the goal of the response is to place students within the disciplines of art history and art criticism by encouraging them to ask and address critical questions (such as "Is this good?"), rather than making them outsiders by presenting these as questions that have already been answered, and devaluing their opinions.

If you don't know the answer to a question, it is always appropriate to say so, and to discuss ways in which students might research the answer. Helping students answer their questions rewards curiosity and encourages them to keep wondering about art and the world.

FACILITATION TECHNIQUES AT WORK

Below are transcripts of three Art Investigations, each of which involves a different artwork. Along with the dialogue, there are notes on how the teacher facilitating the conversation used some of the techniques outlined above. The chapter ends with observations on the use of the facilitation techniques.

Art Investigation 1: "Man, we've got so many ideas!"

This Art Investigation is a particularly good example of the power of encouraging multiple answers. The teacher is also very savvy about when to ask for evidence. The group consisted of second-grade students who were looking at a poster of Marc Chagall's *Green Violinist* (Plate 7).

TEACHER	"What do you notice?" [This question is followed by a long pause.]	*After the teacher asked the question, she waited until students began to answer.*
STUDENT 1	"There's somebody flying in the air like a bird."	
STUDENT 2	"I see a dog and a man. The man looks like he's sweeping."	
STUDENT 3	"The man is different colors, and he's playing a violin."	
STUDENT 4	"There's a green guy who looks like the giant from the book *Abiyoyo*."	
STUDENT 5	"Or the giant from *Jack and the Beanstalk*."	*The teacher let five comments go by without interjecting. In this way the conversation really got rolling, with the students eagerly looking and sharing, and building on each other's comments.*
TEACHER	"Can you say more about why you're saying 'giant'?"	*This interjection asked for evidence, ensuring that the students focused on the painting rather than getting carried away by stories about giants.*
STUDENT 5	"Because he's really bigger than the houses."	
STUDENT 6	"He looks like he's flying—he's playing the violin while he's in the air."	
STUDENT 7	"It looks like he's standing on a house."	
STUDENT 8	"On his left leg there are brown and black squares, and on his right leg black and gray."	
STUDENT 9	"The left side of the pants look like a house and windows."	
STUDENT 2	"Man, we've got so many ideas!"	*The teacher took twelve different observations—with only one interjection—before moving on to the next question.*

Art Investigation 2: "It doesn't look like he used paint."

In this classroom the teacher was able to welcome and value all student answers, while not letting students walk away with incorrect information about the artwork. This Art Investigation was conducted with seventh-grade art students, looking at Cai Guo Qiang's seven-panel *The Vague Border at the Edge of Time/Space Project* (Plate 8).

TEACHER	"What do you notice about this work?"	
STUDENT 1	"It looks like he used tissue paper for the background. It doesn't look like he used paint, more like tissue paper and water."	
TEACHER	"It looks like he used tissue paper and water to you—why?"	*The artist did not use tissue paper, but instead of correcting the student, the teacher tried to uncover what the student is noticing about the work.*
STUDENT 1	"Because it's not as flat as a painting would be, it's more like you could feel it."	
STUDENT 2	"I think the material is like aluminum foil, because it looks so crumply."	
TEACHER	"So some of you are noticing the texture."	*The teacher noted similarities in responses, and that they are about a certain quality of the work (rather than the as-yet-undetermined material the artist used).*
STUDENT 3	"It looks like he might have had a form of the shape of the people, and then he used water to spread it out, because when you spray water or put water on things it makes it run and get more abstract."	
TEACHER	"So you guys are really noticing the artist's balance between controlling things, and then letting things go. As it turns out, Cai made these and dozens of other paintings with gun powder—explosives. He starts with paper, lays out the explosives, and lights them on fire; and then this is the result."	*The teacher told students what the material was, rather than having them guess a "correct" answer.*

Art Investigation 3: "I disagree with my own self."

Chapter 1 included an example of an Art Investigation with Faith Ring-gold's *Tar Beach* (Plate 3). Here we revisit this dialogue to examine the teacher's facilitation of the Art Investigation, and the ways in which this lesson fostered critical thinking skills. These second graders were looking at an overhead projection of the quilt, and had already shared observations of the piece before the conversation recorded here.

TEACHER	"What can we guess about what's happening in this picture?"	
STUDENT 1	"They're looking up at the stars."	
STUDENT 2	"They're eating."	
STUDENT 3	"It might be too cold."	*The teacher let three answers build on each other before breaking into the conversation to ask a follow-up question.*
TEACHER	"Why do you think it might be cold?"	Tar Beach *depicts a summer evening; here the teacher asked for evidence as a way to address an incorrect answer.*
STUDENT 3	[There is a pause.] "I disagree with my own self."	
TEACHER	"It's great how you're taking a deeper look. Go on."	*The teacher vocally valued critical investigation over a correct answer.*
STUDENT 3	"I don't think they're cold, because they're wearing skirts and short sleeves and no socks and shoes."	
STUDENT 4	"But the kid in the bed has blue socks on."	
TEACHER	"Why did you add that?"	
STUDENT 4	"I think the boy is wearing socks because he's little, and the other ones aren't, so they are used to cold and he isn't. And I think one of the family members came up with an idea to see the whole city so they went on the roof and ate."	

STUDENT 5	"On July 4th a lot of people go up on their roof to see the fireworks and they eat dinner on the roof."	
STUDENT 4	"Oh yeah."	*The teacher was allowing the conversation to be among the students.*
STUDENT 3	"I think they're crazy because they brought their bed up on the roof."	
STUDENT 6	"I don't think that's a bed, that's just a mattress."	
TEACHER	[The teacher looks at the image before speaking.] "Does anyone else have any thoughts about this?"	*By looking at the image, the teacher modeled careful looking. By asking students to add onto a debate they have started, the teacher sent the message that disagreement about interpretation is valid, and an appropriate classroom discussion.*
STUDENT 5	"I agree that they're up on the roof, but I don't think that's a bed or a mattress, I think it's just a blanket or a mat they're lying on so that when they're sleepy they don't have to go all the way downstairs to bed and then forget to say something and come back up."	
STUDENT 7	"If they have one bed, how are the parents going to sleep?"	
TEACHER	"Does anyone have any thoughts about that?"	*Here the teacher valued the student's question by echoing it. The teacher could have chosen to explain the narrative of the work (that after dinner the children will move downstairs, where the entire family will sleep in their beds), but this would take the interpretive power away from the students.*
STUDENT 6	"I don't think they're all going to sleep on the roof. I think after dinner they're going to wake up the kids and bring them downstairs, and also I still think it's a mattress, because if you look at the shape, it's kind of three-dimensional."	
TEACHER	"Great. Anything else to add about what's happening in this picture?"	
STUDENT 4	"I think that there is love and peace."	

TEACHER	"What makes you think of love and peace?"

The teacher asked for evidence—particularly important when students extrapolate a mood or concept from a work of art.

STUDENT 4	"Because they are all sitting together, and it looks like they love each other. And what I mean by peace is that they are not fighting and screaming and hitting, and the two children aren't pushing each other off the mat. They're getting along and they love each other."

The conversations in these Art Investigations are unpredictable. The teachers wrote (and stuck with) open-ended questions, and these questions allowed for the conversation, rather than predicting it. The teaching practices of wait time, allowing for multiple answers, asking for evidence, addressing incorrect statements, and addressing student questions were as important to the success of the Art Investigation as the preprepared questions were.

All of these practices are applicable in areas of the classroom beyond Art Investigations. For example, teachers can use both open-ended questions and facilitation techniques in conversations about books or poems, or student artworks, or writing. The facilitation techniques could be used in a math, science, or social studies lesson. Using these techniques across the curriculum consistently shows students their ideas are valued, while reinforcing a classroom climate of curiosity and investigation.

These facilitation skills are not easy to use consistently. As mentioned above, it can be very hard to wait in a silent room for students to begin to answer a difficult question. Open-ended intent is also difficult, particularly in an educational environment that so highly values "correct" answers and high test scores. It takes time to learn these skills, just as it takes time to learn classroom management or lesson planning.

Each of the Art Investigations related above was used in a different classroom context. The conversation about Marc Chagall's *Green Violinist* was a stand-alone conversation, a time for students to come together in dialogue and share an experience, similar to reading aloud to students. Faith Ringgold's *Tar Beach* was used as a jumping-off point for a lesson on local communities. And the art students looking at Cai Guo Qiang's *The Vague Border at the Edge of Time/Space Project* were preparing to create their own artworks that combined control and chance. The next three chapters of this book will explore different contexts in which Art Investigations can further instruction: in the art classroom; integrated with other areas of the curriculum; and as a way to teach critical thinking skills.

Chapter 4

ART INVESTIGATIONS
IN THE ART CLASSROOM

A<small>N ART TEACHER</small> stands in front of a class of third-grade students, while magnets hold a poster of Vasily Kandinsky's painting *Blue Mountain* (Plate 9) on the blackboard. "Take a few minutes to look at this picture," the teacher tells the class, and after waiting a full minute, "Who would like to share something they noticed?" Students quickly share a number of noticings.

"It looks like people riding horses."

"Those could be trees or mountains, and those are definitely people riding horses."

"It's not very clear to me what he was really trying to capture in his mind, because to me it looks blurry and you could probably find other different abstract pictures inside of it."

"For me as a kid it looks like they're on a merry-go-round."

"He used lots and lots of colors."

"In the yellow, if you look closely, there are different colors. And sometimes when you look closely at a color in a painting, it's not just one color."

After the students have shared their initial observations, the teacher says, "The artist who painted this was named Vasily Kandinsky. He created this painting, which he called *Blue Mountain*, 100 years ago. Almost 15 years after he painted *Blue Mountain*, he painted this work." The teacher turns and places a poster of *Composition 8* (Plate 4) next to *Blue Mountain*. "I want you to turn to a partner and talk about the similarities and differences you see in Kandinsky's two paintings." The students talk for a little while, and then the teacher asks, "Would any partners like to talk about what they found that was similar and different?"

"One is abstract, and the other is not abstract."

"In one you can see a lot of shapes, and in the other one there are shapes, but it's harder to find the shapes."

"There are a lot of straight lines in one, and a lot of curvy ones in the other."

"There are rough lines in one, and smooth ones in the other one."

"This one has thinner lines, and that one has thicker lines."

"They're both using different strokes, and the lines go all different directions."

"That one has people, and that one doesn't."

"That blue triangle in the background of *Composition 8* made me think of the blue mountain in the other one, but you can't really tell what's going on in *Composition 8*, and in the other one you can kind of tell what's going on."

"I bet Kandinsky liked a lot of colors, because they both have a lot of colors, and he might like adding different colors, and mixing colors together."

The teacher nods. "You noticed a lot of really interesting similarities and differences between the two paintings. You mentioned how Kandinsky's later painting is more abstract, with clear shapes and lines, and no people or clear story. But you also noticed similarities like the central blue triangles, and the use of lots of colors. Often an artist's work changes over time, but there are some interests or ideas or techniques they keep coming back to. Today we're going to look at some of our own work from the beginning of the year and compare it with the paintings we finished a few weeks ago, to think about what new ideas and skills we have for our art, as well as any themes we notice we keep coming back to."

LOOKING AT ART is a critical aspect of the study of visual arts. By looking at professional works of art, students enter into conversations with the vibrant world of art and artists. The work students do in the classroom becomes part of this larger discipline. Looking at art encourages students to think about how art is made, what they enjoy or what interests them in a work of art, and how people respond to works of art. Looking at art made by others is also part of the work that practicing artists do; by looking at art in the classroom, students further enter into the role of artists. Just as budding writers learn their craft by reading the writings of others, budding artists can learn by looking at what professional artists have created, and how they have used art materials to communicate their ideas and emotions. Accomplished writers read; accomplished artists look at art.

This chapter offers an overview of a particular approach to art education, which is used by the Guggenheim Museum in its Learning Through Art program, situating Art Investigation Methodology within this context. The approach is characterized by the belief that art education should be faithful to the process that artists genuinely engage in. It echoes the Art Investigation

Methodology in its emphasis on open-endedness, independent and critical thinking, and varied and individual interpretations, as well as in its interest in how art is an expression of an artist's ideas and responses to the world.

How do educators engage students in the same processes as professional artists? The work of an artist is to use visual media to respond to and communicate about his or her world. How do artists go about doing this? What processes are common to this work? There are at least five notable processes that artists engage in:

1. Artists spend time learning to manipulate media.
2. Artists explore questions and ideas about the world.
3. Artists become careful observers of the world.
4. Artists make choices related to the expression of ideas and feelings.
5. Artists reflect on and make changes to their art.

It is important to note that people in other (non-art) creative disciplines engage in many of the same processes. Journalists, architects, engineers, designers, teachers, and others learn the techniques of their discipline, explore big ideas about the world, observe carefully, make choices, and reflect. In teaching students to think like artists, you are teaching them to think creatively, in ways that will serve them well in any future creative endeavor.[1]

For each of the five artistic processes listed above, this chapter will both show and discuss an example from the art classroom, and then offer ideas about, and an example of, how Art Investigations can support related student learning.

ARTISTS SPEND TIME LEARNING TO MANIPULATE MEDIA

> For a long time I limited myself to one color, as a form of discipline.
> —Pablo Picasso (*Simpson's Contemporary Quotations*, 1988)

Artists rely on their familiarity and comfort with media to do their work. A ceramicist spends significant time learning to work with clay; a printmaker, even for the simplest types of printmaking, learns the different methods for creating a print plate, as well as how to ink the plate and pull a print. Before they can create art, students also need to experiment with the qualities of clay, ink, paint, or other materials, "to get a feel for that material . . . to learn how to cope with problems engendered by the material so that mastery is secured" (Eisner, 2002, p. 96). This "mastery" is a lifelong pursuit for artists, so students are only beginning, not completing, their lifelong quest to learn what materials might do. After a few sessions, however, students do begin to understand what a material feels like and something about what it can do. With paint, this might include a basic understanding of how it feels to hold a paint brush, how to use the brush in different ways to apply paint on paper, and how colors can be mixed to create new colors as well as tints and shades. Once students have this rudimentary understanding of paint, they can begin to consider how best to communicate through that medium.

In the Art Classroom

Imagine an art teacher facing a class of fourth-grade students. From polling them at the beginning of the week, the teacher knows that most of them have little to no experience with tempera paint, although many have used watercolors. Today is their introduction to this art material. The teacher starts by having them roll up their sleeves and put on smocks. Each student is given paper and a single color of paint; each table has a pile of different sizes and shapes of brushes.

"We're going to start by experimenting with ways to apply paint to paper," the teacher tells them. "Don't worry about what it looks like; we're going to spend the next few months painting, and this is just our first practice. Today we're going to start by using paint brushes to make as many different types of marks as possible." The teacher walks around the room as the students begin to reach for the brushes and dip them in the paint, commenting occasionally on the variety of brushstrokes they are using. When the students have 10 minutes left to work, the teacher adds nontraditional painting implements to the mix—sticks, Q-tips, plastic forks, and sponges. The class ends with students walking around the room looking at their classmates' work to find marks that are different from their own. They also have the opportunity to ask questions of each other.

This is the first painting class; the next week, the teacher will have students experiment with color mixing, ending the class by sharing the colors they mixed and examining the color wheel. In the following class they'll spend some time experimenting with a primary color plus black and white, to make tints and shades. These three classes will provide students with a basic understanding of paint that they can then use in the service of a longer painting project.

Using Art Investigations

During this type of art lesson, Art Investigations can be used to show students the different ways artists have manipulated materials. For example, students might look at a painting in which varied uses of a paintbrush (or other ways of applying paint) are evident. Or they might look at a painting with many variations on one color to discuss how the artist might have mixed the different shades and tints. Art Investigations help link the technical skills students are learning to the larger world of art, by looking at the work artists use these skills to do. An example of an Art Investigation that might support the lesson described above follows.

Art Investigation with Arshille Gorky, *Untitled* (Plate 10)

- What do you notice?
- Pick an area of the painting that interests you; don't tell anyone else what area you are looking at. (Give students a minute to choose an area.) Turn to a person near you and describe your area in as much detail as possible, and see if they can guess what you are looking at.
- Does anyone want to share with the class what area of the painting you selected and what interests you about that area?
- The artist who painted this, Arshile Gorky, used all sorts of unusual techniques to get interesting effects with paint. For the red shape in the bottom left-hand corner, he added turpentine to the paint, which makes the paint thinner—so thin you can see through it—and drippy. Look at the area of the painting you chose. How do you think Gorky might have created the effects in this area?

ARTISTS EXPLORE QUESTIONS AND IDEAS ABOUT THE WORLD

A room hung with pictures is a room hung with thoughts.
—Sir Joshua Reynolds (Edwards, 1915, p. 394)

Art is a way of wondering about and responding to the world. The artist Paul Klee wrote that artists are philosophers; Pablo Picasso wrote that "painting is not made to decorate apartments" but rather art is political (Harrison & Wood, 1999, pp. 348, 640). In both cases, the artists were arguing that art is not an isolated object but a response to the world, that artmaking is a responsive and political activity. Artists do not make art about places, people, or ideas in which they are disinterested; rather, through art they react to things that intrigue them, call out to them, make them wonder.

Artmaking provides students with an opportunity to explore what is important to them. Posing assignments as thoughtful questions rather than commands is an effective way to create the conditions for this exploration. If a teacher tells students to paint their neighborhood, then students may move mechanically through the assignment, making something because the teacher told them to. If a teacher asks students what spaces or structures are essential to their neighborhood community, and spends time supporting student research and exploration in this area, then the artwork, and the process of making art, becomes something more personal and important. By exploring their own ideas about the world and incorporating these ideas and responses into their art, students make connections between their own experiences and ideas, larger areas for exploration, and artmaking.

Encouraging curiosity is an important aspect of teaching students to look at the world as artists. The artist Catherine Opie says,

> My favorite [thing about making art] is the amount of incredible curiosity that I get from looking at the things around me. . . . It's always just this ongoing incredible situation of putting myself in these situations and coming away learning more about who we are in relationship to this world and what we're supposed to be doing as a species, and how to document and reflect that. (Conversations with Contemporary Photographers, Solomon R. Guggenheim Museum, December 2008)

When Guggenheim education staff asked collaborating teaching artists what they wonder about in their own art, answers included: What is the nature of daydreaming? What binds you to a place? How can personal experiences be translated into universal ones? How do people who came before us affect who we are today, and how do we recognize their influence?

Art is the result of interest in or engagement with the world, which can be evoked in the classroom through questions encouraging personal exploration. The engagement of artists with these questions mirrors the engagement educators hope students will find in the classroom. Framing units with questions creates a space in which students can discover their own meaningful connections with the material.

In the Art Classroom

Our fourth-grade teacher wants students to create paintings in response to nature. The choice of this subject area is derived partly from curriculum standards in both art and social studies: Nature, especially as shown in landscapes and still lifes among other genres, has been an important subject of artists throughout the ages; and in their regular classroom the students are learning about Native Americans and thinking about how the Iroquois's relationship with nature was different from or similar to their own relationship to nature. Nature is also an aspect of the world that is both familiar and important to 9-year-olds: It is something that they can engage with in individual ways, experiencing their own curiosity, passion, and intense observation.

The week after the students have their third painting technique class, they walk into the art room to find two questions written on the board: "When in your life have you felt connected to nature? What details, emotions, or specific ideas from this experience are important to you?" As they sit down, the teacher asks them to take out their sketchbooks and to sketch or write in response to these questions. After about five minutes of silent work, students are invited to share their sketches and ideas.

Student answers come slowly and hesitantly at first. One student holds up a sketch of a branch with some flowers on it, saying, "Everyday I pass these pink flowers on the way to school, and they make me feel peaceful and happy."

Another student shows a complicated drawing of a boat filled with people. "I went on a boat ride with my family this summer and saw dolphins swimming next to the boat. They're really fast and cool."

A third student doesn't want to share a sketch, but says, "When our class went to the botanical garden last year we got to plant our own plants, and I still have mine. It's grown a lot because I take good care of it."

After many of the students have shared their ideas, the teacher gives students paper and asks them to fold it in half, and use both sides to sketch four ideas for something related to nature that they might like to paint that would show something about nature that was interesting and important to them.

Using Art Investigations

Art Investigations are critical tools in helping students understand and explore how different artists express different ideas about the world. As students explore their own relationship with nature, the teacher can show examples of how professional artists have made art about the natural world. Here it is important to show a number of examples so that students can see that each artist has a unique response to the natural world, as well as a unique visual style. When students see one way of doing something, they are likely to copy it; when teachers provide multiple approaches, they are likely to find a unique way of approaching the assignment. "Teachers may discuss alternatives and thinking divergently when they demonstrate or introduce a topic, and in doing so they will present children with actual divergent ideas but also suggest to them, even without putting it in words, that creativity is a valuable thing, a worthy thing" (Runco, 2007, p. 189).

For this project, students might look at Joan Miró, *Landscape (The Hare)* (Plate 11); Rufino Tamayo, *Heavenly Bodies* (Plate 12); and Vincent van Gogh, *Mountains at Saint-Rémy* (Plate 6). By posing open-ended questions about these works of art, the teacher can ensure that students consider each as an example of how one artist conveyed something about the natural world, rather than looking at it as an exemplar to be copied. An example of an Art Investigation that explores these ideas follows.

Art Investigation with Rufino Tamayo, *Heavenly Bodies* (Plate 12)

- Take a minute and sketch this painting in your sketchbook.
- What did you notice as you drew?
- What might the figure in this painting be thinking as he looks at this sky?
- The artist who painted this is named Rufino Tamayo, and he painted a number of paintings of the night sky. Why might he have chosen the night sky as a subject?

ARTISTS ARE CAREFUL OBSERVERS OF THE WORLD

> The day is coming when a single carrot, freshly observed, will set off a revolution.
> —Paul Cezanne (Guterman, 1963, p. 329)

Visual artists attend to visual cues in the world. They look carefully, often recording in sketchbooks or through other means the physical appearance of things. Even artists whose work is not rooted in the physical look of the surrounding environment have almost certainly spent significant time trying to sketch or otherwise capture the objects, atmosphere, light, or other elements of their surroundings, or noticing people, places, and events in a careful, perceptive way.

Observing might mean looking carefully at the shape of a leaf or the features of a face, attending to the way the changing light alters the mood of the day, or noticing the patterns that shadows make. Observation is a form of engagement with the world. It helps artists address their questions about the world, and it helps generate new questions about the world.

In the Art Classroom

The fourth-grade teacher wants to make sure students attend to nature before they finalize their ideas and begin their paintings. After they sketch their initial ideas, they are given homework: to keep a record of their encounters with and responses to nature for a week. The teacher encourages them to sketch, write, and even paste photographs, natural specimens, and other items into their homemade sketchbooks.

When students arrive back in the classroom the following week, they share some of their findings in small groups. Then the teacher focuses them on the essential questions for the unit: "What in nature is interesting or important to you? What draws you to that aspect of nature?" After giving them a few minutes to revisit these questions in silence, the teacher tells the class that the rest of the time will be spent sketching and writing from images of nature drawn from image files and nature baskets. Images of trees, flowers, mountains, animals, parks, stones, landscapes, and more are organized in files that are spread out on the desks; baskets of rocks, leaves, pine cones, sticks, shells, and other natural specimens are in baskets on a bookshelf along one wall. The teacher encourages students to look at natural scenes and objects, but also at patterns, tricks of light, colors, and other more abstract elements of nature that inspire them. Students move around the room finding files of images that intrigue them. The rest of the class is spent drawing, as the teacher circulates and conferences with students about new ideas regarding the unit questions, "What in nature is interesting or important to you?" "What draws you to that aspect of nature?" When an image is particularly useful to a student, that student is encouraged to paste the image in a personal sketchbook for future reference.

Using Art Investigations

Art Investigations can be used to support careful observation both through general skill building and through conversations specifically about the role of observation in art. Research has shown that during an Art Investigation students build observation skills. The care with which students look at a work of art and share what they observe is the same care with which, as artists, they need to attend to the world around them. This parallel can be made explicit through assignments such as, "Find something in nature in your home or neighborhood and spend at least 10 minutes looking at it and writing a list of what you notice, just as we did at the beginning of today's Art Investigation." Art Investigations planned to discuss the role of observation in art might investigate what an artist is attending to, the intersection between observation and imagination, or, if comparing two or more works, how different artists attend to different aspects of the world or even different aspects of a particular scene or object. An Art Investigation that explores the duality of observation and choice making in the creation of a work of art follows.

Art Investigation with Vincent Van Gogh's *Mountains at Saint-Rémy* (Plate 6)

- Let's start by trying to describe this painting together as thoroughly as possible.
- This artist, Vincent van Gogh, painted outdoors, observing from nature. Imagine the painter looking at the landscape in front of him and making decisions about what to include in this painting. What are some of the details that you think he might have been observing in the landscape?
- Why might he have chosen to include those aspects of what he was observing?

ARTISTS MAKE CHOICES RELATED TO THE EXPRESSION OF IDEAS AND FEELINGS

> Every good artist paints what he is.
> —Jackson Pollock (Rodman, 1957, p. 82)

The most difficult work of an artist is not the manipulation of media; it is choosing how to use those media to express something that he or she feels is worth expressing. This entails a series of personal choices: What is important to me? What do I want to express about this to others? How can I use the available materials to do this? This expressive quality is what makes art unique. An essential component of good art teaching is helping students understand the power of their own ideas and feelings, and supporting their efforts in finding ways to express these visually.

Teaching that encourages this type of divergent thought is challenging. Traditionally students are all working simultaneously on one area of mastery—for example, every student might be learning about foreground, middleground, and background, or three-point perspective, or gesture drawing. Teaching students in a more individual way requires careful looking and listening, as well as attentiveness to each student's ideas. It requires more time for students to work independently. It requires teachers to embrace and prioritize their work as facilitators, helping students build skills and find ways to make ideas visible.

Teachers will know that students are making choices and cultivating their own artistic vision when each student's artwork is significantly different from his or her classmates. These differences reflect individual choices about subject matter, expression, and materials. Students also signal individual choice making when they consider and reject suggestions and feedback, even those that come from the teacher.

In the Art Classroom

The fourth-grade students are ready to begin their paintings. Students have now chosen the subjects of their paintings by reviewing 2 weeks' worth of sketches, writing, and observations, working independently to put together written or visual proposals for a work of art that addresses the unit questions: "What in nature is interesting or important to you? What draws you to that aspect of nature?" After sharing these proposals with the teacher, students receive high-quality paper and a palette with red, blue, yellow, and white paint (they do not receive black, as most colors can be mixed without it, and students tend to overuse black). As the students work, the teacher circulates and conferences with individual students.

One student is sitting in front of a painting of concentric circles in blue and white. The student is evidently frustrated: arms crossed, mouth turned down. The teacher stoops down and asks about the painting.

"It's water," the student says. "I wanted to show the patterns in water, but this doesn't look like water."

"You've captured some of the patterns with these circles," the teacher responds. "Let's see your sketches."

The student takes out a sketchbook and opens it to a series of pencil sketches of water, including experiments with a few different patterns water makes. Pasted into the book are images of water from magazines, and an artwork, *Still Water (The River Thames, for Example)* by the artist Roni Horn (see Figure 4.1). The teacher notes that the student is very clear about the intended subject—water—and what is interesting about water—the patterns. The student has not yet figured out how to use the medium, paint, to capture this aspect of water.

"You did a fantastic job in your sketches showing these patterns that water makes. It seems like you're having a little trouble translating your ideas to paint—is that right?" the teacher asks. The student nods.

Figure 4.1. Roni Horn. *Still Water (The River Thames, for Example),* 1999 (detail)
15 offset lithographs, each 30 1/2 x 41 1/2" (77.5 x 105.4 cm)
Tate, London
Presented by the American Fund for the Tate Gallery, courtesy of the American
Acquisitions Committee, 2005, accessioned 2008

"One of the advantages of paint is the colors you can get. Here you have some great photographs, and if you look closely, they show lots of different colors in the water, not just blue and white. What do you think about spending some time experimenting with the colors of water, and then you can go back to the patterns once you have some colors you like?"

The student slowly nods. "Should I use this paper?"

"Sure, and there's also a stack of paper over there—the kind we were using to experiment with paints before. You can get more paper from there if you need it."

Using Art Investigations

Art Investigations can help students better understand the choices that artists make, while preparing them to make their own choices as artists. For example, students might look at one of the three paintings mentioned previously—Rufino Tamayo's *Heavenly Bodies,* Vincent van Gogh's *Mountains at Saint-Rémy,* or Joan Miró's *Landscape (The Hare)*—and compare the artist's rendering to a photograph of the same subject. How does Miró's painted landscape differ from a photograph of a landscape with a hare? What is the impact of the choices the artist made? An Art Investigation that allows students to explore an artist's choices follows.

Art Investigation with Joan Miró, *Landscape (The Hare)* (Plate 11)

- What do you notice?
- This painting is called *Landscape (The Hare)*, and it's by the artist Joan Miró. Here is a photograph of a hare, which is like a rabbit. What are some similarities and differences between the hare in the painting, and the hare in the photograph?
- Think of one choice the artist made that interests you. Make a note to yourself about it in your sketchbook.
- Turn to a person next to you and discuss the choices you noticed and why Joan Miró the artist, might have made those choices.
- What are some of the choices that you talked about?

ARTISTS REFLECT ON AND MAKE CHANGES TO THEIR ART

> Perhaps I might be satisfied, momentarily, with a work finished at one sitting, but I would soon get bored looking at it; therefore, I prefer to continue working on it so that later I may recognize it as a work of my mind.
> —Henri Matisse (Barr, 1951, p. 120)

Creating a work of art is generally a lengthy process that entails making, pausing and reflecting, and then adding or changing. To teach students to do the work of an artist involves teaching them to pause and reflect and then return to their work; to spend time making, looking, and returning to making. This alternating between noncritical, creative engagement and a more detached reflective practice is useful not only to artists, but to others who engage in creative work.

In the Art Classroom

During the second class session dedicated to working on their paintings of nature, the teacher asks the students to stop painting 15 minutes before class ends to engage in reflective practice. Students prop their paintings on their chairs, and then move away from their paintings and look at them from different angles. Students are also encouraged to look at the paintings of their nearby classmates. Then they use their sketchbooks to write down at least one thing they like about their painting and at least one thing they want to add, change, or work on during the next session. In the last few minutes of class the teacher asks a couple of students to share things they are interested in changing or adding to their paintings.

"I don't like the color here," says one student, indicating a green patch in the lower left. "It's supposed to look like grass, but it doesn't."

"OK, so next time you'll think about mixing a grass color—or colors—you think might work," says the teacher, making a note. "Let's discuss ways to do that at the beginning of the next class."

Another student offers, "I like how plain my plant is—like it's just the plant, not a whole scene. It looks really strong. I might get rid of this part here so it's really just the plant." The teacher nods.

The student who had earlier struggled to paint water also shares. "I like the greens here—at first I thought I should paint water blue, but I looked at some pictures and I liked the greener colors. I've only just started making the circle patterns, though."

Again, the teacher nods. "We have at least one more day to work on this, so I think you'll have time. Thanks everyone—time to clean up."

Using Art Investigations

Here, Art Investigation techniques can be applied to students' own art. By asking the same observational and interpretive questions about students' art that are asked about professional art, you honor the students' work and process. This challenges them to take their work seriously and to ask meaningful and important questions about the art that they make. In addition, it provides a new lens for them to see their work, as they view it through the eyes of classmates.

When students reflect or comment on their own artwork, or the artwork of classmates, without first taking time for observation, then many of the comments are descriptive, and the conversation often ends without really delving into a deeper analysis of the artwork. Providing a time allotted to looking before the time for interpretive comments and questions allows students to reflect on each other's work more meaningfully. This process also helps student artists become more articulate about what they are doing and why. Even if students cannot fully explain why they chose a certain color or decided to put an object in a particular area of the painting (and many artists do not have language for all of their choices), this process challenges them to begin to think about these choices and their own ways of thinking.

An Art Investigation with student art can be a way to model reflection for the class before students look at their own work in pairs or in small groups. This might be done with a set series of questions related to the project, which are asked in the larger group and then repeated in the smaller group. For example: What do you notice? What do you like about this piece? Have the artist share what he or she was trying to express about what is interesting or important in nature. What is at least one thing that is successful in this piece? What is at least one suggestion you have for the artist?

Alternately, an Art Investigation with a student work can provide time to communally attend to a single student artwork, with the same attention given to professional artworks.

Art Investigation with student artwork (Plate 16)

- Let's describe this artwork as thoroughly as possible. Take a minute to look silently, and then I'll start asking people to share. (Give students 1–2 full minutes to look, and then ask them to begin sharing responses with the class.)
- What are some interesting choices you notice this artist made, and what makes them interesting?
- What might we guess about this artist's ideas about nature?
- Since we are honored to have the artist right here, what questions do you have for this artist? (If possible, give the student artist time to answer questions as they are asked.)

THE GOAL OF most art education programs and classes, particularly at the elementary and secondary school levels, is not to create 30 new artists who will one day see their art displayed at a museum. Rather, it is to teach the students the processes of an artist—manipulating media, exploring questions and ideas about the world, careful observation, meaningful choice making related to the expression of ideas and feelings, and reflection—many of which are the same processes engaged in by non-artists who are curious, engaged, and reflective people. Art Investigations provide a model and a context for this work, and help teach students how to engage in these processes.

Chapter 5

ART INVESTIGATIONS
AND CURRICULUM INTEGRATION

IF YOU TEACH social studies or language arts or science, you may be wondering
how you are going to use Art Investigations in your classroom. How can a
conversation about a work of art further student learning about science, history, or literature? How does an Art Investigation make sense within the small
block of time allotted to your subject in the school schedule?

The school curriculum is broken into subjects intended to reflect real-
world disciplines. Theoretically, it makes sense to consider science as a subject
in which you would teach the ways in which scientists approach and examine the world. Those who argue for disciplinary divisions believe that this
approach ensures the integrity of each subject being taught. However, any
school subject is a pathway to multiple real-world disciplines. For example,
there are many careers in which people use science, and in each job the practi-
tioners approach and examine the world differently: Consider research physi-
cists, engineers, and science journalists. Moreover, people in one field often
look to subject matter from another field: Historians might read the literature
of an era to better understand that era, while scholars of literature read the history of that era to better understand the literature. There are also more global
ways of viewing the world that encompass multiple disciplines: The ecological
phenomenon of global warming is best understood when considered along
with the scientific and technological advancements, economic pressures, and
sociological changes that both contribute and respond to global warming.
The compartmentalization of subjects is also problematic in that it prevents
schools from teaching psychology, philosophy, engineering, computer science,
and other areas of study that do not fit neatly into the prescribed knowledge
areas.

Curriculum integration brings multiple school subjects together in some
way. Non-art-related examples include reading historical fiction while studying that era in social studies, or framing math problems to challenge students

to solve problems similar to those of that same era. Curriculum integration makes many art educators nervous because historically "art integration" has often meant using art or art materials to in some way enliven teaching in other areas. For example, teachers might have students paint portraits of historical figures, or make Egyptian-style cartouches with their name in hieroglyphics, or build models of molecules using modeling clay and toothpicks. The problem with these activities, from the perspective of an art educator, is that the students learn very little about art from the experience.

When art is used to support learning in another area, it is considered a "subservient approach" to curriculum integration. Ideally, subjects are brought together on more "coequal" footing, where both disciplines are being attended to (Bresler, 1995). Coequal curriculum integration is a challenging prospect, as it means attending to multiple sets of goals and types of learning at once. It is worthwhile, however, because while a subservient approach to integration teaches students that the arts are fun and nonessential to real learning, a coequal approach demonstrates the real work of artists, modeling new ways to explore and relate to the world and communicate ideas. As with any subject, if you choose to include the arts in your classroom, it is important to present them in a meaningful way.

The visual arts are genuinely and deeply connected to other school subjects. Art is not created in a vacuum; it is created in response to a culture, ideas, and other works of art. Artists make art that is about something—sometimes about art or materials, but more often about the same subjects that fuel all human thought: cultural or personal beliefs, intriguing ideas, people, or places. Because art is a way of communicating, rather than a prescribed content, there are countless ways that looking at art can inform teaching in other subjects, while teaching related to other subjects can inform students' understanding of art.

So what might coequal integration of art and other subjects look like? The Guggenheim's Learning Through Art program uses a framework that starts with large, open, multidisciplinary questions, called "essential questions" by Grant Wiggins and Jay McTighe in their influential book *Understanding by Design* (1998). These are questions that are relevant to students as well as the disciplines being studied. Examples of essential questions that have framed Learning Through Art projects include "What are the traits of a good leader?" "What is worth taking a stand for?" or "What is an ideal community?"

For example, in exploring "What is worth taking a stand for?" fifth-grade students looked at people throughout history who took a stand for something they thought was important. Students interviewed community members about issues of importance to them and thought about what they personally believe is worth taking a stand for. They also looked at how artists and graphic designers use visual tools to convince people that something is worth taking a stand for. Ultimately, the students made their own posters for causes that they felt were important.

This chapter focuses on three areas of overlap between visual arts and other school subjects. First, artists consider and respond to ideas related to different disciplines. Second, artists' work reflects their culture. Third, visual artists work with elements common to other arts, including literature. For each area of overlap, a discussion of the topic is followed by an example of what this vision of integration might look like in the classroom and suggestions for how Art Investigations might support this learning. These examples are hypothetical, featuring teachers with the time and freedom to collaboratively plan engaging and deep curricula. However, even for teachers in schools where the reality is too little planning time, prescribed curricular objectives, the pressure of looming tests, and other barriers to this type of planning and teaching, these snapshots provide concrete demonstrations of how Art Investigations can support student learning in any classroom. In addition, they offer the opportunity to consider what a truly integrated curriculum might look like.

ARTISTS CONSIDER AND RESPOND
TO IDEAS RELATED TO DIFFERENT DISCIPLINES

Artists address ideas from nearly all areas of human experience. A quick look through the Solomon R. Guggenheim Museum's *Collection Online* (2009) reveals art that addresses twentieth-century theories about space and time (Pablo Picasso, *Accordionist*, summer 1911), apartheid (William Kentridge, *History of the Main Complaint*, 1996), cities and government housing (Marjetica Potrc, *Kagiso: Skeleton House*, 2000–01), slavery (Kara Walker, *Insurrection! Our Tools Were Rudimentary, Yet We Pressed On*, 2000), social dynamics (Rirkrit Tiravanija, *untitled 2002 (he promised)*, 2002), and much more. Often, artists articulate their explorations in terms that directly relate to other disciplines.

The artist Matthew Ritchie is interested in the overlap between ideas in different disciplines and considers both science and social issues in his work:

> I start with a collection of ideas. . . . So I was thinking about the idea of the cell. In biology, it's the sacred unit of measurement; the whole body's built out of the cell. . . . Robert Hooke discovered and named the cell around

1780. He was really thinking about it as a chamber. He looked into the body, saw all these little rooms, and imagined that these animalcules living inside had this whole civilization. So I'm very interested in questions of *scale*, how big or small does something have to be to feel confining? (Ritchie, n.d.)

In an interview, the artist Louise Bourgeois discussed her use of geometry, demonstrating a deep understanding of the subject area and its symbolic possibilities:

Geometrical figures, circles, half-circles, points, lines, vectors . . . were my vocabulary and still are today. The basis of Euclidean geometry is that parallels never touch. . . . Euclidean or other kinds of geometry are closed systems where relations can be anticipated and are eternal. It comes naturally to me to express emotions through relations between geometrical elements. (Bloch, 1976, p. 372)

And artist Kara Walker described a piece in the Guggenheim's collection and its relationship to the history of slavery in the United States:

Well, this piece is called *Insurrection! Our Tools Were Rudimentary, Yet We Pressed On.* . . . The idea at the outset was an image of a slave revolt at some point prior to me. And it was a slave revolt in the antebellum south where the house slaves got after their master with their instruments, their utensils of everyday life. (Walker, n.d.)

These artists explore ideas in a deep and meaningful way. While their processes are each unique and probably nonlinear, they clearly include identifying ideas or questions of interest to them, finding ways to understand the subject more deeply, making decisions about what information to attend to, and envisioning a visual product that relates to new knowledge and insight. These artists provide models for students of ways to engage with the world of ideas in a personal and meaningful way. They also model how students might incorporate the world of ideas into their own creations, whether in visual art, writing, performing arts, or other endeavors.

In the Classroom

Imagine a group of eighth graders wondering, "What is an ideal community?" In social studies they are learning about the founding of the United States of America, and considering what the founding fathers believed an ideal community was and whether they achieved it. In English they are reading

Lord of the Flies and discussing what went wrong in the community founded by the group of children in this book. In art class they are communally envisioning and painting their ideal community. In math class they are discussing and learning some of the math people would need to create the societies they are envisioning in their art class.

Using Art Investigations

Near the end of the unit, the social studies teacher shows students a number of contemporary ideas about ideal communities. Later, students will be asked to write a paper examining in what ways American ideas about an ideal community have changed since 1776. One of the artworks the teacher shows students is Andrea Zittel's *A–Z Wagon Station, Customized by Russell Whitten*, 2003 (Plate 13). The teacher asks the students:

- What do you notice?
- This is *A–Z Wagon Station*, a work of art that is also a living space. Inside are a mattress and a shelf, and it was created as a living space for the desert in California. The entire front of the *Wagon Station* can flip open. What do you think it would feel like to be inside this piece?
- The artist who created this piece, Andrea Zittel, created a number of these *Wagon Stations*, as well as a number of other pieces reenvisioning how people might live today. She thinks a lot about individual space, human needs, and community. Imagine living in a community in which everyone lived like this. What would work well about that way of living? What problems would people encounter?
- As best you can tell from this artwork and the information I have shared, in what ways do Zittel's ideas about community reflect American founding ideals? In what ways do they challenge these ideals?

ARTISTS' WORK REFLECTS THEIR CULTURE

Looking at a people's artistic output is a critical aspect of understanding any culture. Works of art often capture the physical appearance of a place and time. They also capture the ideas of a culture, sometimes referred to as the *zeitgeist*.

The art historian Michael Baxandall (1988) notes, "An old picture is the record of visual activity. . . . Approached in the proper way . . . the pictures become documents as valid as any charter or parish roll. . . . [by observing aspects of the work of painters] we are observing something not only about them but about their society." Often works of art provide visual information about clothing, architecture, and other aspects of material culture. The painting *Hermitage at Pontoise* by Camille Pissarro (Plate 14) offers visual evidence about life in the nineteenth century. Faith Ringgold's *Tar Beach* (Plate 3) shows a more recent scene of life in New York City, letting the viewer glimpse what an evening on the roof of a city building might be like.

Works of art also share information about the beliefs, rituals, and values of cultures. It is hard to imagine studying ancient Egypt without looking at pyramids or hieroglyphics, or ancient China without studying paintings, calligraphy, or architecture. The Aztec piece cited in Chapter 1 (Figure 1.1) helps us to understand how Aztecs thought about time and aging. Art "reflect[s] the moral or intellectual climate in which it was produced" (Collins, 1991). Artists in the late nineteenth century began painting the lower class in a sympathetic manner—previously rare in most European traditions—demonstrating concern for the growing working class in the newly industrialized, urban world. These paintings are examples of a new genre in art mirroring a new concern in society.

Art is a record of both what societies are like and how people responded to them. By viewing and discussing the artistic output of a culture along with other information and documentation, students can see tangible evidence of how societies are similar to or different from their own. They can understand how artists respond to the societies in which they live. By considering the artistic output of our own culture, students can reflect on the concerns, values, and beliefs of the twenty-first century and their own responses as citizens and possibly as artists.

In the Classroom

A group of third-grade students is exploring the question, "How does technology change the way we live?" Their teacher developed this question in part to encourage students to be thoughtful about the amount of time they spend watching television and playing video games and about the possibilities offered by the computer and Internet. Their social studies class is dedicated to local history, so they are looking at how their own East Coast town has changed from the days before European settlers arrived until the twenty-first century. Each student is also picking an everyday object—paperclip, computer, book, and so on—to research with the help of resources provided by the teacher, finding out when that object was invented, why it was invented, and how (or if) it changed people's lives. In language arts they are reading fantasy books in which children travel to different times or places, and they will write their own fantasy stories about traveling to the past. In science these students are learning about electricity: They are making a battery with lemons, learning about the ways we use electricity in our lives, and comparing it to other energy forms. With their art teacher, students are inventing new forms of everyday objects—drinking vessels, chairs, bags, and shoes—that are designed with their own lives, as well as imagined future technology, in mind.

Using Art Investigations

One of the paintings the teacher uses to explore the question "How does technology change the way we live?" is Camille Pissarro's painting *Hermitage at Pontoise* (Plate 14). For the Art Investigation with this painting, the teacher's goal is to have the students understand that life was different 150 years ago, largely because of the technology that has been invented in the past 150 years. The teacher has written the following Art Investigation plan:

- Take some time and look carefully at this painting. A few minutes later: What do you notice?
- Imagine that we entered this painting. You walk up to the poster, you look at it, and suddenly you are inside this scene, looking around. Notice what you see, hear, smell, feel. What does it feel like to be in this place?
- This was painted in 1867 by the artist Camille Pissarro, and it shows us the French town he lived in, Pontoise. Why might Pissarro have chosen this town to paint over and over—what might Pissarro have wanted to show us about this town?
- Imagine that you could visit this place in the twenty-first century. Knowing how much the world has changed since 1867, how do you think Pontoise might be different today?

This Art Investigation transports students to another time and place. A vivid image, like a vivid story, paired with a multisensory prompt, helps students imagine themselves in a new place, time, or situation. The communal nature of Art Investigations allows the teacher to work with the group in practicing this exercise of the imagination, pushing students to consider the sensory experience of being elsewhere. Student responses can also help teachers identify and correct any misconceptions about this alternate space; for example, if students looking at *Hermitage at Pontoise* say they hear cars in the distance, a teacher can (kindly) remind students that cars have not been invented yet.

While the Art Investigation above, like the others in this book, explores a work from the Guggenheim Museum's collection, a wide range of primary sources might be used to explore a culture or historical era. Visual primary source documents include photographs, advertisements, maps, political cartoons, and other material that is often collected by art museums and displayed as art. These documents, particularly when viewed in the context of an Art Investigation, can be wonderful ways to offer students insight into events, time periods, and cultures they might be studying.

As part of the unit on "How does technology change the way we live?" and the examination of how daily life has changed over the past 150 years, this resourceful third-grade teacher also looks at digital collections from respected sources such as the Library of Congress and university libraries. The class examines early-nineteenth-century photographs of cities across the United States (found on the Teachers page of the Library of Congress Web site at http://www.loc.gov/teachers), considering questions that echo the discussion with *Hermitage at Pontoise*: What do you notice? What most interests you about this scene? What do you think a photographer 100 years ago might have been interested in when looking at this scene? What might this photographer have been trying to capture? How do you think this place is different today?

The teacher also shows the students images of early-twentieth-century advertisements from the Duke University Libraries Digital Collection (http://library duke.edu/digitalcollections). They look closely at advertisements for food and compare these with advertisements for food printed in contemporary magazines, which the students found and brought in as homework. Looking at the older advertisement, they ponder these questions: How is this advertisement similar to or different from this other advertisement from a recent magazine? What evidence do these two advertisements offer for changes in our eating habits or food production methods over the past century? What thoughts do you have about these changes? As with all Art Investigations, these questions are open-ended and relate both to the works under examination and to students' own lives.

VISUAL ARTISTS WORK WITH ELEMENTS
COMMON TO OTHER ARTS, INCLUDING LITERATURE

Because reading and writing are essential and common communication tools in our world, and because reading is a skill that must be learned (as it involves decoding otherwise-meaningless symbols called *letters*), language arts has a special place in the school curriculum. One result of this is that the art form of literature is taught even when no other art forms are taught in a school, and the ability to understand a work of literature is considered important even by those who think the arts otherwise unimportant. Yet literature is an art form, and many philosophers, art historians, and literary critics have dedicated countless pages to discussing the similarities and differences between the literary and visual arts. Both are "symbol systems humans employ . . . to describe and understand the world and their experience of it" (Maine, 1999, p. 43). Both use these complex symbol systems to capture a vision of reality and explore ideas about human existence.

The author and artist grapple with similar questions in their work: How can I capture something important about the world or about life to share with others? How can I say it in an interesting, profound, and/or beautiful way? Similarly, the reader and art viewer, including professionals (the professor of literature or literary critic in one field, the art historian or art critic in the other), grapple with similar questions: What does this work say to me? How does it achieve this?

Many of the questions of the language arts curriculum have parallels in the visual arts curriculum: How do artists and writers use symbolism? How do artists and writers convey character or place? How does one successfully tell or show a story? What references is the artist or writer alluding to in this piece?

In the Classroom

Seventh-grade students are thinking about symbolism. Their teachers have posed the essential question, "How do symbols communicate an idea?" In language arts they are reading poetry, identifying poets' uses of symbols, and thinking about what these symbols communicate, as well as writing their own poetry. In art they are painting symbolic self-portraits using animals or animal traits. In dance class they are choreographing dances that build on symbolic body language. In math class they are thinking about the symbols used in mathematics, and in social studies they are thinking about the ways in which governments use symbols to communicate.

Using Art Investigations

The language arts teacher is planning to have students read Alastair Reid's poem "Curiosity" and Billy Collins's poem "Dharma," both of which use dogs and cats symbolically. Students will then write their own poetry in which an animal is used as a symbol for a personality trait. Collaboratively, the language arts teacher and the visual arts teacher identify three works of art to look at with students that relate to both the visual and language arts projects and that introduce conversations about a range of animals and their possible symbolism: Louise Bourgeois, *Maman* (Plate 15); Pierre Auguste Renoir, *Woman with Parrot* (see Figure 5.1); and Franz Marc, *Yellow Cow* (see Figure 3.1). For the conversation with Bourgeois's *Maman*, the teachers ask the following questions:

- What do you notice?
- What words or moods do you associate with this image, and why?

Figure 5.1. Pierre Auguste Renoir.
Woman with Parrot
(La Femme à la perruche), 1871
Oil on canvas
36 1/4 x 25 5/8 inches (92.1 x 65.1 cm)
Solomon R. Guggenheim Museum, New York
Thannhauser Collection, Gift, Justin K. Thannhauser 78.2514.68

- This sculpture is called *Maman*, which means mother. The artist, Louise Bourgeois, often creates art that symbolizes aspects of her family and childhood. What do you think this sculpture might tell us about her feelings about her mother?

After students complete their poems and paintings, the visual art and language arts teachers jointly lead a class in which they ask students to talk about the differences in using symbols visually and through language. They also explore the range of symbolic qualities that students were able to draw from their chosen animals, and reflect on the work itself.

This chapter has described and modeled various ways that the visual arts can be integrated with other curricula in a coequal manner. The overarching questions for all of the sample units drew on genuine areas of intersection between the arts and other subjects: the ways in which artists explore ideas, the ways art reflects the time and place in which it was made, and the elements, such as symbolism, that visual art has in common with literature and other art forms. For many teachers, this way of thinking about the curriculum may be appealing but unrealistic. How do you find the time to plan with the other teachers on your grade level? Is it possible to redesign the curriculum into integrated units? For teachers working in schools where true curriculum integration is a daunting prospect, Art Investigations focused on integrating art with one other subject can be a manageable first step. Art Investigations provide an opportunity for your own explorations about how art can be integrated with the curriculum, allowing you to consider how an Art Investigation might simultaneously contribute to your proscribed subject matter and teach students something about art.

Chapter 6

ART INVESTIGATIONS
AND CRITICAL THINKING

OVER A **4-YEAR** period beginning in the fall of 2003, education staff from the Guggenheim Museum worked with a team of evaluators to look at the impact of its Learning Through Art program on students' critical thinking skills.[1] We suspected that students who engage in Art Investigations learn how to think critically about art, and we wondered if these skills transferred—if improved art-related critical thinking skills would be evidenced in other domains. To measure the development and transfer of these skills, we decided to compare students who participated in Learning Through Art with their peers who did not, testing both groups' critical thinking skills in response to a reproduction of a painting and an excerpt from a written text. To determine which skills were applicable to thinking about both a work of art and a text, we gathered a team of art and literacy experts to guide us. After participating in an Art Investigation and engaging in weeks of discussion, this team identified six critical thinking skills to examine: extended observation, thorough description, hypothesizing, giving evidence, understanding multiple interpretations, and schema building.

This research, conducted during the school years 2004–06 with 565 students in four New York City schools, showed that the Learning Through Art program improved students' critical thinking skills in five out of the six targeted areas for each domain tested (art and literacy). Interestingly, the area in which students did not do better than their peers was different in analyzing an artwork and analyzing a text: For art, the area was thorough description; for text it was schema building. It is unclear, therefore, if schema building—making connections between new information and prior knowledge—transfers between domains. The researchers and educators involved in this project all attributed the students' improved abilities to analyze art and texts to one particular aspect of Learning Through Art: students' regular participation in Art Investigations, which were led by teaching artists in the classrooms once each week for 20 weeks. It is likely that all Art Investigations contribute to the development of these skills, whether focused on artmaking skills, social studies or science content, the students' own lives, or a political issue of the day.

The Guggenheim's findings are supported by other research conducted around inquiry-based methodologies for looking at art. A methodology called Visual Thinking Strategies has been found to improve students' critical thinking skills (Institute for Learning Innovation, 2007); evidentiary reasoning skills cultivated through this methodology appear to transfer to the realm of science (Project Zero, 1999). Other museums, such as the Wolfsonian Museum at Florida International University, and arts education academics, such as David Perkins from Harvard University's Project Zero, have also made claims that looking at art can foster these skills (Rawlinson, Wood, Osterman, & Sullivan, 2007; Perkins 1994).

Critical thinking is extremely hard to teach because it is knowledge—bound—you need to know information about something in order to think about it (Willingham, 2007). To learn critical thinking skills in a social studies context, for example, students need to learn a fair amount about a specific time and place in order to think critically about that information. While the arts have their own sets of contextual information to be studied, a work of art is often intended to be considered and reacted to as a discreet unit, without the need for additional context. This is true of a dance, a poem, or a painting. Any of these can be thought about in a meaningful way without learning information beyond what is apparent in the work of art itself.

Among these art forms, visual art has a few distinct advantages. First, works of visual art are complex and rich but, unlike a written text, do not require decoding of alphabetic symbols. Second, works of visual art are usually perceived by students as nonthreatening and engaging; often, students who may frown or sigh with dismay when confronted with a text are very happy to be asked what they notice or think about a work of art. Third, many works of art are contained and static—a group of 30 students can simultaneously observe the entire piece. If a child refers to a patch of color or a facial expression within the painting, there is no page flipping to find the reference and no need to think back to an earlier part of the performance.

As discussed in Chapter 1, there are many reasons to look at and discuss art that have nothing to do with critical thinking skills. These skills, however, are essential to understanding a work of art: "The prow of the Tanimbarese boat needs a long and thoughtful look, not just the passing glance, to begin to understand its message and savor its elegance" (Perkins, 1994, p. 3). In developing students' critical thinking skills, you are developing their ability to view and interpret a work of art.

Within the larger scope of K–12 education, improving critical thinking skills is an important goal for all students. In fact, we might argue that in the K–12 classroom learning any discreet discipline or knowledge set is always less important than learning the cognitive skills that will allow children to grow into adults who can seek out, consider, and apply new knowledge as they need it. It is important, therefore, to consider the role that art can play in teaching these essential and complex skills.

This chapter outlines the six critical thinking skills that the Guggenheim's research demonstrated can be cultivated through Art Investigations. For each of these skills, I explain why the skill is important to the two domains studied—art and literacy—and how Art Investigations support the development of this skill.

OBSERVATION SKILLS:
EXTENDED FOCUS AND THOROUGH DESCRIPTION

Students exhibiting *extended focus* take the time to look carefully at what they are reading or looking at. They demonstrate this by including detail in their description of what they have read or seen and by asking questions about what they are noticing. Students who give a *thorough description* of a work are specific in their descriptions and directly reference what they have read or seen, including thinking about how the text was written or the artwork was created. Someone who listens to a thorough description can fully understand what the student read or was looking at.

These skills are important to understanding both art and texts because one must perceive before one can truly comprehend. All too often people make assumptions about what they think they are looking at without looking carefully. Students sometimes fail to attend to what they are reading or being read: In *Mosaic of Thought* (1997) Ellin Oliver Keene and Susan Zimmerman describe a classroom in which, as the teacher read a book aloud, "children were looking out the window; others played with little pieces of paper or pencils, others stared vacantly as if they didn't know how to listen" (p. 34). Learning to attend is an essential part of learning to understand and think critically.

Art Investigations build observation skills because they consistently begin by asking students to spend time noticing and sharing what they see. They give significant time to this task, allowing students to linger and look for a while before moving on to an interpretive question. *Wait time*—asking a question and then waiting for a number of students to share their ideas—is critical to this lingering. A good example of extended observation and thorough focus was included in Chapter 3, in the inquiry in which third-grade students looked at Mark Chagall's painting *Green Violinist*:

> "What do you notice?" (This question is followed by a long pause.)
> "There's somebody flying in the air like a bird."
> "I see a dog and a man. The man looks like he's sweeping."
> "The man is different colors, and he's playing a violin."
> "There's a green guy who looks like the giant from the book
>   *Abiyoyo*."
> "Or the giant from *Jack and the Beanstalk*." . . .
> "He looks like he's flying—he's playing the violin while he's in the
>   air."
> "It looks like he's standing on a house."
> "On his left leg there are brown and black squares, and on his right
>   leg black and gray."
> "The left side of the pants look like a house and windows."
> "Man, we've got so many ideas!"

This Art Investigation was successful at developing extended observation and thorough description skills because the teacher allowed the students significant time to notice what was in the painting. Also, the teacher waited until the students had described much of what was in the picture before asking an interpretation question. If a casual observer heard this discussion but could not see the painting the students were looking at, he would have a great deal of information about what the painting looks like. Allowing for this abundance of observational findings to be shared helps students learn to fully examine the properties of a work of art, text, natural object or phenomenon, or other material under discussion before moving on to analyze what the material might mean.

INTERPRETATION SKILLS:
HYPOTHESIZING, EVIDENTIARY REASONING, BUILDING SCHEMA,
AND UNDERSTANDING MULTIPLE INTERPRETATIONS

Students who are skilled at *hypothesizing* offer specific and viable explanations that make meaning from what they are reading or looking at. In other words, they pose good guesses about why something might be the way it is. If they are also skilled at *evidentiary reasoning*, they then offer support for their hypotheses through sharing relevant evidence drawn directly from the text or image.

Hypothesizing and evidentiary reasoning are similar to the literacy skill of *inferring,* which is defined in *Mosaic of Thought* (Keene & Zimmerman, 1997) as a skill set including predicting, answering questions, making connections, and making analytical judgments, which happens when students "create a meaning that is not necessarily stated explicitly in the text" (p. 162). Deanna Kuhn, a cognitive psychologist, similarly defines *inferring* as answering the question, "What can I claim and how do I know?" (Kuhn, 2005, p. 88).

Hypothesizing and evidentiary reasoning take readers beyond perception and into comprehension. For example, a child who is skilled in this area can read the book *Tar Beach* by Faith Ringgold, and understand that the protagonist, Cassie, is a dreamer and likes New York City, even though nowhere in the book does it explicitly state these facts (Keene & Zimmerman, 1997, pp. 156–157). Equally important is that student's ability to explain *how* he or she knows that Cassie is a dreamer and likes New York City. Students need to be able to explain how they know what they know because it is this self-knowledge that ensures careful and accurate interpretations (Kuhn, 2005, p. 77).

For an example of both hypothesizing and evidentiary reasoning with a work of art, we return to our fifth-grade students from Chapter 1, in front of Edgar Degas's *Dancers in Green and Yellow.* "I . . . think they're going to go on stage soon, because usually when someone goes on stage they kind of look a little nervous, and it looks like some of them are doing stretches." As with the student reading *Tar Beach* and inferring ideas about Cassie's personality and interests, the students here have transformed their observations of four dancers posed against a patterned background into a hypothesis about the context of this scene. Art Investigations teach hypothesizing by posing truly open-ended questions that ask students to interpret works of art. These questions allow students independence in forming hypotheses: Rather than second-guessing the teacher, students are engaged in the genuine work of trying to form an explanation for why something is the way it is. As a follow-up to these hypotheses, teachers leading Art Investigations explicitly ask students for evidence from the artwork to back up their assertions (often in the form of a question along the lines of "What are you noticing in the artwork that makes you say that?"), thus cultivating evidentiary reasoning. As Lucy Calkins (2001) points out, when "others repeatedly say to us . . . 'What in the text makes you say this? Where's your evidence?' then we, as readers, begin to ask these questions of ourselves" (p. 226).

Schema refers to the way one understands the world. When students engage in *schema building,* they make strong connections between their explanations of the artwork or text and prior knowledge and/or personal experience. These connections are logical and specific.

Connecting new information with the known is the way people make sense of and remember things. The cognitive scientist Daniel Willingham (2006) wrote in an article for teachers:

> New material is more likely to be remembered if it is related to what is already in memory. Remembering information on a brand new topic is difficult because there is no existing network in your memory that the new information can be tied to. But remembering new information on a familiar topic is relatively easy because developing associations between your existing network and the new material is easy. (Willingham, 2006)

For example, a gardener introduced to a new flower is more likely to remember its name, family members, and care instructions than a nongardener who knows little about plants. Similarly, a child who already knows something about sharks is likely to better understand and remember a story about a shark than is a child who has never thought about sharks previously. Keene and Zimmerman (1997) note that schema building has long been recognized as an important aspect of literacy.

In an Art Investigation, a successful line of inquiry is one that offers students opportunities to make connections between the artwork and what they already know. This helps them make personal meaning from a work that hundreds of people may have viewed slightly differently before them. For example, in the Art Investigation of Mark Chagall's *Green Violinist* cited in the previous section of this chapter, the third-grade students made connections between the main figure in the painting—the green violinist, who appears larger than the houses and the other figures in the painting—and characters they remembered from literature: Abiyoyo, from Pete Seeger's song and book of the same name, and the giant from the story *Jack and the Beanstalk*. In another Art Investigation, cited in Chapter 5, a student looking at a Kandinsky painting makes a connection between the intentional blurriness of the painting and the way the world looks from a whirling playground structure, saying, "For me as a kid it looks like they're on a merry-go-round."

Comparing the figure of the green violinist to giants from literature allows students to begin making sense of what it might mean for one figure to be so much larger than the others. Noting that a blurry effect in painting recalls the experience of a quickly passing landscape allows a student to understand blurriness as speed. By using these connections to lead into more explicit hypothesizing and evidentiary reasoning, the teacher can begin to help the students decide whether these connections help them better understand the paintings or whether new ideas need to be generated to better interpret the art.

Schema building did not appear to transfer from the art to the literacy realm. However, it was clear that students who engaged in Art Investigations were better at schema building than their peers in the art realm. One explanation of why this skill did not transfer is that students are accustomed to creating schema in response to texts already. Thus students who did not participate in Learning Through Art are still able to demonstrate good skills related to schema building. Perhaps making connections is a skill that students need only the opportunity to engage with in order to do it well.

Students who understand the concept of *multiple interpretations* understand that alternate interpretations of a text or an artwork are possible. They exhibit this understanding by revising or adding to their explanations in such a way as to generate new ideas. They also use phrases that reveal their awareness of subjectivity, such as "I think," "possibly," or "one way to think of it is."

The recognition that others might interpret texts differently is important to literacy because it helps students refine, question, and enrich their ideas about a text. Students who believe that the way they initially understand a text or image must be correct are not able to allow flexible and sophisticated thinking to blossom in response to classroom discussion. Literacy expert Lucy Calkins cites the example of a student conversation in which students are challenged to agree or disagree and to elaborate on others' ideas as one in which students learn to learn from conversations (Calkins, 2001, pp. 233–238). This, of course, requires a willingness to listen to and consider multiple interpretations of a single text. Beyond literacy, the ability to tolerate, weigh, and respond to new interpretations is a central skill for a citizen engaging in any dialogue.

Art Investigations work to build this understanding in many ways. After asking a question, teachers wait for multiple answers to the question, demonstrating to students that there is not a single correct answer, but rather many ways of addressing the question posed. The interpretive questions themselves are open-ended and challenging, welcoming alternate and sometimes opposing answers. Teachers let students puzzle out the meaning of the work of art by acting as facilitators rather than instructors, encouraging a productive communal dialogue.

In an Art Investigation with Marc Chagall's *Paris Through the Window* (Plate 2), a teacher asked third-grade students how the painting made them feel. The answers were varied and, with prompting, supported:

"I feel a little scared."

"What makes you feel that way?"

"I feel scared because of the cat's face, and I wouldn't want to be
on a train upside down. And that man with two faces, one side is
blue and the other side is freaky and scary."

"I feel kind of sad, because really the face on the cat looks pretty sad.
I don't really think the people are flying, I think they're lying on
the ground."

"Maybe they're floating or something."

"I sort of have a weird feeling, and I sort of have a cool feeling."

"Why does this make you feel cool?"

"I feel sort of calm, and I think it's weird though. It's cool that the
person has two heads, the cat looks like it has a person's face, the
train is upside down, the colors in the background."

"So you think it's cool for the same reasons that other people might
feel scared by this painting."

Through this dialogue, the teacher cultivated students' awareness that people
can respond in different ways to a single work of art. This understanding—
that different people perceive and react to things in different ways—is not just
an academic skill, but a life skill as well.

THESE ARE THE SIX critical thinking skills that research shows Art Investigations cultivate: extended observation, thorough description, hypothesizing, giving evidence, schema building, and understanding multiple interpretations. By engaging in Art Investigations, students learn how to think carefully and critically about art. By thinking carefully and critically about art, students learn how to think.

CONCLUSION

IN ORDER TO share the Art Investigation Methodology, this book has attempted to codify this educational strategy. It has boiled down planning an Art Investigation into clear steps and suggested very specific ways that this methodology can support learning in a variety of subjects.

It is both necessary and dangerous to codify an educational methodology. To teach a new skill or way of doing things, one needs to be specific: Here is how you cook a chicken; here is how you craft a persuasive essay. The initial lessons need to be concrete enough to offer the skills and confidence one needs to begin to move into action.

But teachers are individuals, classrooms are vibrant and unique communities, and mandates and ideas about best practices are ever changing. Effective educational strategies must be flexible and responsive to the needs of the teacher and student, as well as to the educational priorities of a place and time. This is both a challenge and an opportunity. The best cooks and writers invent new ways of doing things, pushing their fields ever forward.

I hope that you can find this flexibility within your own practice of using Art Investigation Methodology and discover new ways to push student interactions with art forward, advancing the field. These changes and advances should be rooted in the core values that are at the heart of this educational practice and should not be compromised: Art is valuable to society and education. Inquiry is an essential teaching strategy as well as a way of approaching the world. Individuals and communities are capable of making sense of the world both individually and together.

It is surprising, really, that these values are not shared more broadly. Why do American schools not see art as more central to either learning about cultures and histories or evidencing and teaching successful thinking skills? Perhaps it is because success in art is seen to be untestable, and anything that is not tested easily falls by the wayside in a time when accountability is the watchword in society. Perhaps it is because artists are most successful when they do the unexpected, and our society has always been ambivalent about the unexpected: Who do we want to surprise us, and who do we want to do what they are told? What role do we want the unexpected to play in our public schools?

Inquiry as an educational methodology has been taking hold for some time. Unfortunately, it is hard to practice genuine inquiry when working toward a test in which there is one right answer. Working together, perhaps the professions can convince schools that students cannot be good scientists, good art historians, good writers, good mathematicians, good artists, good managers, or good teachers if they do not know how to pose and contemplate open-ended questions. Perhaps together we can imagine new vehicles for accountability that do not do battle with the values of inquiry.

Just as our society is ambivalent about hoping for the unexpected, we are ambivalent in our expectations for and interest in individuals and communities making their own sense of the world. The world is an easier place to communicate and work in when people understand it in similar ways; new understandings lead to revolution (slavery is bad; women should be able to vote; everyone should have health care; low-income parents should have the same range of school choice that their wealthier counterparts do). In his introduction to the English translation of *Pedagogy of the Oppressed*, by the radical Brazilian educator Paulo Freire, Richard Shaull (1997) notes:

> Education either functions as an instrument which is used to facilitate integration of the younger generation into the logic of the present system and bring about conformity *or* it becomes "the practice of freedom," the means by which men and women deal critically and creatively with reality and discover how to participate in the transformation of their world. (p. 16)

Conformity is safer than the "practice of freedom," but also more limiting. As educators, we need to decide whether we are integrating children into a set of predetermined beliefs or offering them the tools to create their own world. It is not clear to me that we can do both. Artists, while not a single identifiable political or educational group, are often individuals who have aligned themselves with the latter position, creating powerful statements about and against contemporary ways of being.

Opening up the classroom to art, and particularly to art in an open-ended context, is both essential and problematic. This book clearly endorses a vision of educators as professionals who can and should teach students to think for themselves and reinvent their world. Art has a critical role to play in making our classrooms into brave and open communities that endorse these new ways of thinking.

INFORMATION ABOUT THE ARTISTS AND ARTWORK FEATURED IN PLATES 1–15

The biographical and artwork-specific information presented in this appendix is adapted from the Solomon R. Guggenheim Museum's *Collection Online* and other Guggenheim source material. The original authors include curators Jennifer Blessing, Vivien Greene, Ted Mann, Alexandra Monroe, Nancy Spector, and Michelle Yun; art historians Lucy Flint and Cornelia Lauf; editor Meghan Dailey; and educator Chelsea Frosini.

Plate 16 features student work; we have not included information about this piece.

PLATE 1: EDGAR DEGAS (1834–1917)

Degas was born in 1834 in Paris to a wealthy banking family. After studying law briefly, he turned to art, spending time in the Louvre studying and learning by copying art. Later he traveled to and lived in Italy.

Degas exhibited with the Impressionist artists during the 1870s and 1880s. Like many of the Impressionists, he was interested in scenes from daily life. Many of his subjects were drawn from the lower classes, including his laundresses and ballerinas. Toward the end of his life Degas's sight began to fail, but he continued to draw with pastels and to sculpt wax molds for bronzes. Degas died in 1917.

Dancers in Green and Yellow (1903)

Edgar Degas is considered a master of drawings of the human figure in motion and of capturing the psychology of his subjects through their physical expression. His preferred drawing medium was pastel, a type of crayon made with pigments ground into a paste. Pastels allowed Degas to draw quickly and capture small moments that would be over before a full painting could be completed. He used pastels more and more as his vision began to fail in the mid-1880s.

In *Dancers in Green and Yellow*, thought to be one of the artist's later pastels, the broad marks and less finely modeled figures suggest that Degas was really experimenting with the medium. Degas had begun to concentrate on the theme of the female ballet dancer in the early 1870s. Unlike today where work in the ballet is considered an elite profession, in the nineteenth century ballerinas were frequently women from the lower classes who often relied upon the patronage of their wealthy male admirers.

PLATES 2 AND 7: MARC CHAGALL (1887–1985)

Marc Chagall was born in Vitebsk, Russia. From 1907 to 1910 he studied in Saint Petersburg, Russia, at the Imperial Society for the Protection of the Arts. In 1910 he moved to Paris. Chagall visited Russia in 1914 and was prevented from returning to Paris by the outbreak of war. He settled in Vitebsk, where he was appointed Commissar for Art in 1918.

During World War II Chagall fled to the United States, then settled permanently in France in 1948. During the 1960s Chagall continued to travel widely, often in association with large-scale commissions he received. Among these were a window for the United Nations building in New York (installed in 1964) and murals for the New York Metropolitan Opera House (installed in 1967). Chagall died on March 28, 1985, in Saint-Paul-de-Vence, France.

Paris Through the Window (1913)

For Marc Chagall, the Eiffel Tower served as a metaphor for Paris and perhaps modernity itself. Chagall's parachutist might also refer to contemporary experience, since the first successful jump occurred in 1912. Other motifs suggest the artist's native Vitebsk. The two-faced man in *Paris Through the Window* has been read as the artist looking at once westward to his new home in France and eastward to Russia. Chagall, however, refused literal interpretations of his paintings, and it is perhaps best to think of them as lyrical evocations.

Green Violinist (1923–24)

In *Green Violinist* Chagall evoked his homeland. The artist's nostalgia for his own work was another impetus in creating this painting, which is based on earlier versions of the same subject. His cultural and religious legacy is illuminated by the figure of the violinist dancing in a rustic village. The Orthodox Judaism of Chagall's childhood believed it possible to achieve communion with God through music and dance, and the fiddler was a vital presence in ceremonies and festivals.

PLATE 3: FAITH RINGGOLD (1930–)

Faith Ringgold was born Faith Willi Jones in the Harlem neighborhood of Manhattan. Her mother, a fashion designer and seamstress, encouraged Ringgold's creative pursuits from a young age. Ringgold earned a bachelor's degree from City College of the City University of New York in 1955. She then taught art in New York City public schools, which she continued to do until 1973.

During the late 1960s and the 1970s Ringgold played an instrumental role in the organization of protests and actions against museums that had neglected the work of women and people of color. Her artwork of that time also carried strong political messages in support of the civil rights movement. More recently, she has come to embrace the potential for social change by undermining racial and gender stereotypes through impassioned and optimistic presentations of black female heroines.

Ringgold's vehicle is the story quilt, a traditional American craft associated with women's communal work that also has roots in African culture. She originally collaborated on the quilt motif with her mother, a dressmaker and fashion designer in Harlem. That Ringgold's great-great-great-grandmother was a Southern slave who made quilts for plantation owners suggests a further, perhaps deeper, connection between her art and her family history.

Tar Beach (1988)

Tar Beach, the first quilt in Ringgold's colorful and lighthearted series entitled *Woman on a Bridge*, depicts the fantasies of its spirited heroine and narrator Cassie Louise Lightfoot, who, on a summer night in Harlem, flies over the George Washington Bridge. "Sleeping on Tar Beach was magical. . ." explains Cassie in the text on the quilt, "only eight years old and in the third grade and I can fly. That means I am free to go wherever I want to for the rest of my life." For Ringgold, this phantasmic flight through the urban night sky symbolizes the potential for freedom and self-possession. "My women," proclaimed Ringgold about the *Woman on a Bridge* series, "are actually flying; they are just free, totally. They take their liberation by confronting this huge masculine icon—the bridge."

Ringgold adapted the story quilt *Tar Beach* for an eponymous children's book published in 1991. Its critical and popular success led to her development of several other titles for children. For adults, she wrote her memoirs, published in 1995.

PLATES 4 AND 9: VASILY KANDINSKY (1866–1944)

Vasily Kandinsky was born in 1866 in Moscow. He studied law and economics at the University of Moscow. In the 1890s he went to Munich, Germany to study art. In 1911

Kandinsky began to exhibit with a group called Blaue Reiter; that same year, his book *On the Spiritual in Art* was published. He lived in Russia from 1914 to 1921, principally in Moscow, where he held a position at the People's Commissariat of Education.

Kandinsky began teaching at the Bauhaus, an art and design school in Germany, in 1922. He became a German citizen in 1928. The Nazi government closed the Bauhaus in 1933 and later that year Kandinsky settled in France; he acquired French citizenship in 1939. Fifty-seven of his works were confiscated by the Nazis in the 1937 purge of "degenerate art." Kandinsky died on December 13, 1944, in Neuilly, France.

Blue Mountain (1909)

Vasily Kandinsky's use of the horse-and-rider motif symbolized his crusade against conventional aesthetic values and his dream of a better, more spiritual future through the transformative powers of art. The rider is featured in many of Kandinsky's woodcuts and paintings.

In 1909, the year he completed *Blue Mountain,* Kandinsky painted no less than seven other canvases with images of riders. In that year his style became increasingly abstract and expressionistic and his thematic concerns shifted from the portrayal of natural events to apocalyptic narratives.

Composition 8 (1923)

While teaching at the Bauhaus, Kandinsky furthered his investigations into the correspondence between colors and forms and their psychological and spiritual effects. In *Composition 8,* the colorful, interactive geometric forms create a pulsating surface that is alternately dynamic and calm, aggressive and quiet. The importance of circles in this painting prefigures the dominant role they would play in many subsequent works. "The circle," claimed Kandinsky, "is the synthesis of the greatest oppositions. It combines the concentric and the eccentric in a single form and in equilibrium. Of the three primary forms, it points most clearly to the fourth dimension."

PLATE 5: KIKI SMITH (1954–)

Kiki Smith was born on January 18, 1954, in Nuremberg, Germany, the daughter of sculptor Tony Smith. Brought up in South Orange, New Jersey, she enrolled at Hartford Art School in Connecticut in 1974, but dropped out 18 months later. Settling in New York City in 1976, Smith earned her living over the next few years doing odd jobs. Around 1978 she joined an artists' collective devoted to making art accessible through exhibitions outside commercial gallery settings. It was during this period that she made her first artworks, monotypes of everyday objects. Virtually self-taught, Smith describes herself as "a thing-maker."

In 1985, propelled by an interest in obtaining practical knowledge about the body, Smith studied to become an emergency medical technician. For most of the 1980s and into the 1990s, Smith's work focused primarily on the human body. In the 1990s she shifted focus to the animal kingdom, especially birds, whose ferocity and vulnerability echo the human condition.

Ribs (1987)

In 1979 Smith turned to the reference book *Gray's Anatomy* as a source for drawings that depict aspects of the human body in cross section and on a microscopic level. A few years later she produced sculptures of body parts and internal organs made of paper, plaster, resin, and various metals. Representations of the human circulatory and nervous systems followed. In her transition from exploring the body's interior to its exterior, Smith began to investigate the skin as a system and subsequently to create visceral, life-size figures (usually female).

Smith's delicate sculpture *Ribs* represents in terra-cotta the components of a rib cage, strung together and held up like a marionette suspended from the wall. The pink rib bones, disconnected from the sternum, some revealing repaired breaks, imply forensic evidence of trauma. The apparent fragility of Smith's piece evokes the transience of life itself. *Ribs* registers the passage of time both in the way that the unique rendering of the bones suggests that they might have belonged to a specific individual, and the manner in which its display evokes the natural history museum and its fascination with the organic specimen as a link to a collective past.

PLATE 6: VINCENT VAN GOGH (1853–1890)

Vincent van Gogh was born in 1853 in Groot-Zundert, the Netherlands. Beginning in 1869, he worked for a firm of art dealers and at various short-lived jobs. While working as an evangelist in a poor mining district in Belgium, he decided to become an artist. His early subjects were primarily peasants depicted in dark colors. He lived in Brussels and in various parts of the Netherlands before moving to Paris in February 1886. In Paris he lived with his brother, Theo, and encountered Impressionist and Postimpressionist painting. He began painting flowers, portraits, and scenes of Montmartre; he also began using a brighter palette.

In February of the following year van Gogh moved to Arles, France, where he painted in isolation, depicting the Provençal landscape and people. Paul Gauguin joined him in the fall, and the two artists worked together. In December of 1888, after the two artists had a falling out, van Gogh suffered his first mental breakdown. Numerous seizures and intermittent confinements in mental hospitals in Arles, Saint-

Rémy, and Auvers-sur-Oise followed from that time until 1890. Nevertheless, he continued to paint. Van Gogh shot himself on July 27, 1890, and died on July 29 in Auvers-sur-Oise, France.

Mountains at Saint-Rémy (July 1889)

During the years preceding his suicide in 1890, Vincent van Gogh suffered increasingly frequent attacks of mental distress, the cause of which remains unclear. *Mountains at Saint-Rémy* was painted in July 1889, when van Gogh was recovering from just such an episode at the hospital of Saint-Paul-de-Mausole in the southern French town of Saint-Rémy. The painting represents the Alpilles, a low range of mountains visible from the hospital grounds.

Van Gogh advocated painting from nature rather than inventing a motif from the imagination. On a personal level, he felt that painting outdoors would help to restore his health, a sentiment he often voiced when writing to his brother, Theo. Nature had a quasi-religious or transcendental significance for van Gogh. In the face of industrialization and modernization (the Eiffel Tower was built the same year that this canvas was painted), van Gogh longed nostalgically for a rural environment peopled with good-natured, God-fearing peasants.

PLATE 8: CAI GUO-QIANG (1957–)

Cai Guo-Qiang was born in 1957 in the Fujian province of China. He studied stage design at the Shanghai Drama Institute and emerged as a member of China's experimental art movement that burgeoned in the early 1980s postreform era. He moved to Japan in 1986, and has been based in New York since 1995.

Cai is best known for his use of gunpowder, which was invented by the Chinese as an elixir of immortality; Cai mines its identification with China, original medicinal use, and ongoing equation with violence. Explosives are central to Cai's signature gunpowder drawings, which are made by igniting gunpowder on fibrous paper, leaving the charred residue of the original matter. Gunpowder is also the essential material for his explosion events, which are outdoor, site-specific pyrotechnic displays, often on a monumental scale.

The Vague Border at the Edge of Time/Space Project (1991)

In this gunpowder drawing Cai attempts to elucidate the fluid relationship between seen and unseen worlds and, more specifically, to pinpoint "the vague border at the edge of time/space" where the two worlds meet. His quest for an understanding of this dichotomy within the universe and the indistinctness of the border at which these two realms intersect and overlap, giving rise to a world of ambiguity, is fundamental to his working practice and is a topic on which he focuses much energy. This drawing is self-reflective. The life-size figures depicted on each of the seven panels were created by using daylight to project the artist's own shadow onto the paper.

PLATE 10: ARSHILE GORKY (1904–1948)

Arshile Gorky was born Vosdanik Adoian in the village of Khorkom, province of Armenia, on April 15, 1904. Gorky left Armenia in 1915 and arrived in the United States in 1920. He stayed with relatives in Watertown, Massachusetts, and with his father, who had settled in Providence, Rhode Island. In 1925 he moved to New York and changed his name to Arshile Gorky. From 1935 to 1937 he worked under the WPA Federal Art Project on murals for Newark Airport.

From 1942 to 1948 he worked for part of each year in the countryside of Connecticut or Virginia. A succession of personal tragedies—including a fire in his studio that destroyed much of his work, a serious operation, and an automobile accident—preceded Gorky's death by suicide on July 21, 1948, in Sherman, Connecticut.

Untitled (1944)

Arshile Gorky spent the greater part of 1944 at Crooked Run Farm in Hamilton, Virginia, where he produced a large number of drawings, many of which were conceived as preliminary studies for paintings. This work is preceded by such a study. Landscape references appear in *Untitled*; though the white ground is uniform, it is empty at the very top of the canvas, suggesting a slice of sky, while the "earth" below is replete with vegetal shapes and floral colors. A clear gravitational sense is produced by the dripping of paint thinned with turpentine.

PLATE 11: JOAN MIRÓ (1893–1983)

Joan Miró Ferra was born April 20, 1893, in Barcelona, Spain. At the age of 14, he went to business school in Barcelona and also attended art school in the same city. Upon completing 3 years of art studies, he took a position as a clerk. After suffering a nervous breakdown, he abandoned business and resumed his art studies. In 1920 Miró made his first trip to Paris, after which he divided his time between Paris and Montroig, Spain. Miró died on December 25, 1983, in Palma de Mallorca, Spain.

Landscape (The Hare) (1927)

In *Landscape (The Hare)*, Miró returned to one of his favorite subjects, the countryside around his family's home in Catalonia. Miró said that he was inspired to paint this canvas when he saw a hare dart across a field on a summer evening. In *Landscape*

(The Hare) this event has been transformed to emphasize the unfolding of a heavenly event. A primeval terrain of acid oranges and red is the landscape in which a hare with bulging eyes stares transfixed by a spiraling comet.

PLATE 12: RUFINO TAMAYO (1899–1991)

Rufino Tamayo was born on August 26, 1899, in Oaxaca, Mexico. Tamayo began taking drawing lessons in 1915 and by 1917 had left school to devote himself entirely to the study of art. In 1921 he was appointed head of the Department of Ethnographic Drawing at the Museo Nacional de Arqueología in Mexico City, where his duties included drawing pre-Columbian objects in the museum's collection. Tamayo integrated the forms and slate tones of pre-Columbian ceramics into his early still lifes and portraits of Mexican men and women.

Tamayo taught for 9 years, beginning in 1938, at the Dalton School in New York. In 1957 he settled in Paris, where he executed a mural for the UNESCO Building in 1958. Tamayo returned to Mexico City in 1964, making it his permanent home. He died in Mexico City on June 24, 1991.

Heavenly Bodies (1946)

Rufino Tamayo filtered his pre-Columbian heritage through the pictorial tradition of European Modernism in images of man's confrontation with the forces of nature and the universe. In several paintings of 1946–47 he showed primitive figures gesticulating in terror, awe, or longing at the patterns of astral and planetary orbits.

The lines traversing the sky in *Heavenly Bodies* may represent light emanating from stars or the tails of meteors or may also indicate the mental constructs that join stars in constellations. These lines dissect the rich blue sky into flat planes and simultaneously provide the illusion of movement through a vast space. The purity of the sky's geometry is contrasted with the unevenly curving contours of the human figure, associated formally with the earth. A setting sun is evoked by the red strip on the hill and is reflected on the man's face.

PLATE 13: ANDREA ZITTEL (1965–)

Andrea Zittel was born in California in 1965. She received her MFA in sculpture from the Rhode Island School of Design, and then moved to New York. While working in an art gallery, Zittel began designing her own clothes, which became her *A–Z Six-Month Personal Uniforms*. This was among the first of her experiments in reconceptualizing and designing tools for living. Her work now includes living spaces, furniture, and food.

In 2000 Zittel moved to the Mojave desert in California and created what she calls "A–Z West," a studio space and home. She considers A-Z West "an institute of investigative living," and says, "The A-Z enterprise encompasses all aspects of day-to-day living. Home furniture, clothing, food all become the sites of investigation in an ongoing endeavor to better understand human nature and the social construction of needs." Zittel is also involved in providing events and spaces in which other artists can share their work.

A–Z Wagon Station (2003)

Since the early 1990s Zittel has been designing alternative structures for living under the guise of her fictive one-person corporation, A–Z Administrative Services. For her *A–Z Wagon Stations*, begun in 2003, Zittel developed temporary living shelters that reference both the covered wagons of the old western frontier and the standard suburban station wagons of today. Although the *Wagon Stations* do not have wheels, they are easy to collapse, transport, and reassemble. Their small size allows them to evade building codes, providing the inhabitant with the potential for greater freedom and autonomy. As with Zittel's prior designs, the *Wagon Stations* are "customized" in various ways by their users. A number have been adapted by artists and other individuals for use at A–Z West, the experimental live/work compound Zittel founded in 2000 in the desert near Joshua Tree, California. The *Wagon Station* pictured here was customized by Russell Whitten, a longtime desert resident and dirt bike enthusiast, who painted the exterior with a hot rod design of red flames and employed it as a rest station at A–Z West.

PLATE 14: CAMILLE PISSARRO (1830–1903)

Jacob "Abraham" Camille Pissarro was born on July 10, 1830, to French Jewish parents on the West Indies island of Saint Thomas. Sent to boarding school in France, he returned after 6 years to work in his parents' store. Pissarro abandoned this comfortable bourgeois existence at the age of 22, when he left for Caracas, Venezuela.

After returning briefly to Saint Thomas, Pissarro left in 1855 for Paris, where he studied art. Working in close proximity with artists later associated with the Impressionist movement, he began to revise his method of landscape painting, privileging the role of color in his expression of natural phenomena and employing smaller patches of paint.

After moving briefly to London, Pissarro settled in Pontoise, France. Pissarro lived long enough to witness the start of the Impressionists' fame and influence. In the last years of his life, Pissarro experienced eye trouble, which forced him to abandon outdoor painting. He continued to work in his studio until his death in Paris on November 13, 1903.

The Hermitage at Pontoise (1867)

The view represented in this painting is a winding village path at the base of a cluster of houses in Pontoise, France, known as the Hermitage. Camille Pissarro lived there on and off between 1866 and 1883, choosing the rural environs of the provincial capital for a series of large-scale landscapes that have been called his early masterpieces. Pissarro's idyll, replete with villagers and neatly tended gardens, is more than just the naturalist painter's attention to perceived reality. It is a continuation of the French academic landscape tradition.

PLATE 15: LOUISE BOURGEOIS (1911–)

Louise Bourgeois was born on December 25, 1911, in Paris. As a teenager, Bourgeois assisted her parents in their tapestry-restoration business, making drawings that indicated to the weavers the repairs to be made. In 1932 she entered the Sorbonne to study mathematics, but abandoned that discipline for art. In the mid- to late 1930s, she studied at various Parisian art schools. In 1938 Bourgeois married an American, the art historian Robert Goldwater, and moved to New York. Thirteen years later, Bourgeois became an American citizen.

Bourgeois first gained notice in the 1940s with her Surrealist-inspired *Personnages*: thin, vertical forms in wood or stone that evoke the human body. Installed in clusters, suggesting a small crowd or perhaps a family, the *Personnages* were meant to symbolize figures from the artist's past.

Through a vast oeuvre spanning over 60 years, Bourgeois has plumbed the depths of human emotion further and more passionately than perhaps any other artist of our time. In its evocation of the psyche, her work is both universal and deeply personal, with frequent, explicit reference to painful childhood memories of an unfaithful father and a loving but complicit mother. With the rise of feminism and the art world's new pluralism, her work found a wider audience. Many of her large-scale works have been exhibited as public art, including three spider sculptures installed at Rockefeller Center in New York in 2001 under the aegis of the Public Art Fund.

Maman (1999, cast 2001)

Like a creature escaped from a dream, or a larger-than-life embodiment of a secret childhood fear, the giant spider Maman casts a powerful physical and psychological shadow. Over 30 feet high, the mammoth sculpture is one of the most ambitious undertakings in the long career of Louse Bourgeois. *Maman* is associated with the artist's own mother. The spider, who protects her precious eggs in a steel cage-like body, provokes awe and fear, but her massive height, improbably balanced on slender legs, conveys an almost poignant vulnerability.

ADDITIONAL ART INVESTIGATION PLANS

The Art Investigations in this appendix were written to suit a variety of classrooms, subjects, and age levels. They may need slight adaptation to meet your specific classroom needs. All are written for the images included in the color plates in this book.

Each Art Investigation is titled with a teaching point: the area of understanding that this Art Investigation is intended to support. Also indicated are the appropriate grade levels and relevant curriculum areas—art (A), English language arts (ELA), social studies (SS), or science (Sci). Where the teaching point indicates that students will understand something about artists, you are encouraged to make connections between the work of visual artists and literary artists (authors).

Edgar Degas, *Dancers in Green and Yellow* (Plate 1)

Some artists want to offer people new ways to think about the world

Grades 4-8; A, ELA, SS

- Take a few minutes to look carefully at this work. (Wait a few minutes while students look.) What do you notice?
- This pastel drawing was created by an artist named Edgar Degas. What do you think was interesting to him about these dancers backstage?
- Sometimes artists want to offer people new ways to think about certain things. What new ideas do you think Degas might have wanted to share with people?

Artists show aspects of character through gesture

Grades 2–8; A, ELA

- What do you notice?
- Pick one of the dancers to focus on. What can you guess about her personality?

97

- The artist, Edgar Degas, was very interested in drawing people in motion. He believed that how people thought and felt could be captured through their physical expression. Try to stand in the same way as one of the dancers in the picture. Now try to bring this person to life. What more can you guess about her personality by moving like her?

Marc Chagall, *Paris Through the Window* (Plate 2)

Different communities have similarities and differences

Grades 2–5; SS

- What do you notice?
- This painting is called *Paris Through the Window,* and the artist was living in Paris when he painted it. What does the painting show us about Paris?
- Compare this place to your own neighborhood. What's similar? What's different?

Artists can use color to communicate ideas and emotions

Grades 4–8; A

- What do you see?
- What do you notice about the colors the artist used?
- Some people think the man in the bottom right-hand corner represents the artist, Marc Chagall, looking both east toward Russia, where he was from, and west toward Paris, where he lived when he painted this piece. How might Chagall have felt about both of these places?
- If students have not yet discussed the role of color in conveying ideas and emotions, How do his choices of colors communicate these ideas and emotions?

Faith Ringgold, *Tar Beach* (Plate 3)

Point of view matters to how you understand a scene

Grades 2–5; ELA

- What do you notice?
- What can we guess about what is happening in this picture?
- Why might the artist have depicted a girl flying?
- The girl flying is the narrator of this story, Cassie. She is also pictured lying down on the roof. Imagine this scene from her point of view.

What might Cassie want to tell us about the people and the place in this painting?

Artists choose media and materials purposefully

Grades 3–8; A

- Turn to a partner and, together, try to name everything you see in this picture.
- What did you notice?
- Artists make art in lots of media—for example, paintings, drawings, or sculptures. This is a *story quilt,* a format which this artist, Faith Ringgold, has used in her art since 1980. We only have one story quilt to look at today, but she has made a number of them. Looking at this piece, what can we guess might be important features of story quilts?
- Why might the artist have used this format for her artwork?

Vasily Kandinsky, *Composition 8* (Plate 4)

Descriptive language is an important way to understand art

Grades 3–8; ELA, A

- Let's describe this painting together, as though we were talking to someone who couldn't see the painting and wanted to know all about it.
- If we were going to pick some words that this picture reminds us of, what words might we choose?
- I have here a list of some words and phrases a curator used to describe this painting (Spector, 2009):
  —Calm, but dynamic
  —Aggressive and quiet
  —Pulsating
  Why do you think she chose these words, and do you agree or disagree?

Kiki Smith, *Ribs* (Plate 5)

Science and art use similar source material in different ways

Grades 6–8; Sci, A

- Take a look at the artwork represented here. (Allow for at least one full minute of silent looking.) What do you notice?
- This picture (show picture) is from Henry Gray's *Anatomy of the Human Body,* an anatomy book that the artist, Kiki Smith, looked at as a model for *Ribs.* In what ways is her sculpture similar to or different from

this sketch of human ribs? (See Figure 2.4 for an illustration).

- The artist who created the illustration of the ribs from *Gray's Anatomy* was trying to create the clearest, most accurate image possible as a resource for doctors. Kiki Smith clearly had a different goal, and made different choices. Why might Kiki Smith have chosen to depict ribs, and why might she have made the choices she did?
- Take a minute and sketch an idea for your own artwork that uses some part of the human body to convey a message or idea about human existence.
- Compare your ideas to Kiki Smith's. Do you have any new thoughts on *Ribs*?

Vincent van Gogh, *Mountains at Saint-Rémy* (Plate 6)

Artists attend to specific elements in nature, chosen for particular and personal reasons

Grades 3–8; A, SS

- Let's start by trying to describe this painting together with as much detail as possible.
- This artist, Vincent van Gogh, often painted outdoors, observing from nature. Imagine the painter looking at the landscape in front of him and making decisions about what to include in this painting. What are some of the details you think he might have been observing in the landscape?
- Here is a picture of a mountain [or river, or field] near here. (Show students a picture of a natural landscape element in your community.) If you were going to paint a picture of this, what about it would you most want to capture?
- With this in mind, do you have any new thoughts about this painting by van Gogh?

One place or source can convey different moods

Grades 3–8; A, ELA

- What do you see?
- Take a moment to think about how it might feel to step into this painting. What moods does the painting suggest to you, and why? Share your responses with the rest of the class. (Record students' responses on a T-chart.)
- We have listed different, contrasting moods. Can you think of any places you know that make you feel different moods at different times?

Artists use brushstroke intentionally and creatively

Grades 4–8; A

- What do you notice?
- Let's focus for a minute on describing the brushstrokes in this painting.
- What would it would feel like to be in this place?
- Let's go back to the brushstrokes, which we talked about earlier. How do they affect our ideas about how it might feel to be in this place?
- The artist, Vincent van Gogh, wrote a letter to his brother as he was working on this painting. He said, "They will tell me that mountains are not like that and that there are black outlines of a finger's width." He knew that others would think his brushstrokes were unrealistic, but he chose to paint like this anyway. Why might he have chosen to use these types of brushstrokes?

Marc Chagall, *Green Violinist* (Plate 7)

Communities have traditions and celebrations that are important in many ways

Grades 3–5; SS

- What do you notice?
- What can we guess about the main figure?
- What can you guess about where he is?
- Violinists often played at ceremonies and festivals in this artist's native country. What might we guess about how the artist felt about these violinists and their role in the community?

Fantasy and reality are genres that artists use strategically and sometimes combine

Grades 3–5; ELA, A

- Let's work together to list everything in this picture as thoroughly as possible.
- This artist, Marc Chagall, often combined real and imaginary elements. What in this picture seems realistic? What seems imaginary? Explain your answers.
- Why might the artist have chosen to create this particular combination of fantasy and reality?

Cai Guo-Qiang, *The Vague Border at the Edge of Time/Space Project* (Plate 8)

Note: Cai Guo-Qiang works with a very unusual method and material—he explodes gunpowder to create "drawings" and events. His process can be viewed on the *Art: 21* Web site, at http://www.pbs.org/art21/artists/cai/index.html#

Some artists use chance as part of their artmaking practice

Grades 5–8; A

- With a partner, pick one of the panels and describe it.
- What did you notice?
- Cai Guo-Qiang created this artwork by exploding gunpowder onto paper. While he carefully arranges the powder and fuses, he has chosen a material that leaves a lot to chance. Why might an artist choose a material that they could not fully control?

Artists explore ideas in their art, including (sometimes) ideas related to science

Grades Grades 6–8; A; Sci

- What do you notice?
- Each of these panels is a silhouette of a human figure. What are some of the differences between the seven panels?
- The artist, Cai Guo-Qiang, works with gunpowder as a material. He arranges the powder and fuses carefully on paper and then explodes it. In this piece he used this method to capture his own shadow seven different times. I have here five different words; with a partner, take one of these words and discuss how it might relate to the piece. (The words are: *vague, border, edge, time, space.* You may want to write them on index cards—with enough cards for each pair of students—and hand each pair a card.)
- What did you discuss?
- The title of this piece is *The Vague Border at the Edge of Time/ Space Project.* We have already talked about most of these words in connection with this piece. Using this title to guide us, what might the artist be exploring in this piece?

Vasily Kandinsky, *Blue Mountain* (Plate 9)

> Artists' styles change over time, but some elements of their practice remain consistent

Grades 3–5; A

- Take a few moments to look at this picture. (Wait at least one minute while students look.) Who would like to share something they noticed?
- The artist who painted this was named Vasily Kandinsky. He created this painting, which he called *Blue Mountain*, 100 years ago. Almost 15 years after he painted *Blue Mountain*, he painted *Composition 8*. Turn to a partner and talk about the similarities and differences you see in Kandinsky's two paintings.
- Would any partners like to talk about what they found that was similar and different?

> A work of art often shows a single moment, and we can use clues in the image to imagine what came before and what will come after

Grades 3–5; ELA

- What do you notice?
- What seems to be happening in this painting?
- Imagine this scene as a single snapshot of a longer story. What might have happened right before this? What will happen afterward? Write or draw your ideas.

Arshile Gorky, *Untitled* (Plate 10)

> Painters use a variety of often experimental techniques to get different effects

Grades 3–8; A

- What do you notice?
- Pick an area of the painting that interests you; don't tell anyone else what area you are looking at. (Give students a minute to choose an area.) Turn to a person near you and describe your area in as much detail as possible, and see if they can guess what you are looking at.
- Does anyone want to share with the class what area of the painting you selected, and what interests you about that area?
- The artist who painted this, Arshile Gorky, used all sorts of unusual techniques to get interesting effects with paint. For the red shape in

the bottom left-hand corner, he added turpentine to the paint, which makes the paint thinner—so thin you can see through it—and drippy. Look at the area of the painting you chose. How do you think Gorky created the effects in this area?

Joan Miró, *Landscape (The Hare)* (Plate 11)

Artists make purposeful choices about what to include, ignore, and transform in their art

Grades 3–8; A, Sci

- What do you notice?
- This painting is called *Landscape (The Hare)*, and it's by the artist Joan Miró. Here is a photograph of a hare, which is like a rabbit. What are some similarities and differences between the hare in the painting and the hare in the photograph?
- Think of one choice the artist made that interests you. Make a note to yourself about it in your sketchbook.
- Turn to a person next to you, and discuss the choices you noticed, and why Joan Miró, the artist, might have made that choice.
- What are some of the choices that you talked about?

Art can provide inspiration for our own imaginative stories

Grades 3–5; ELA

- Let's take a look at this piece. What do you notice?
- What might be happening in this picture?
- The artist said a few things about this painting: the creature is a hare, which is like a rabbit, and the dots represent the sun, but also a falling comet. Now that we know this, do we have new ideas about what might be happening in this piece?
- Write a story that might go with this painting.

Rufino Tamayo, *Heavenly Bodies* (Plate 12)

Artists are purposeful about choosing subjects for their art

Grades 5–8; A, ELA

- Take a minute and sketch this painting in your sketchbook.
- What did you notice as you drew?
- What might the figure in this painting be thinking as he looks at this sky?

- The artist who painted this is named Rufino Tamayo, and he painted a number of paintings of the night sky. Why might he have chosen the night sky as a subject?

Constellations are invented by humans to make sense of the night sky and vary from culture to culture

Grades 3–8; Sci

- What do you notice about this painting?
- Some people think that one of the subjects of this painting is the way people have invented ways to connect stars into constellations, or patterns. What do you notice about how the stars are connected in this painting?
- How are the constellations in Tamayo's painting similar to or different from constellations you are familiar with?

Andrea Zittel, *A–Z Wagon Station* (Plate 13)

Different people have different ideas about what an ideal society looks like

Grades 5–8; SS

- What do you notice?
- This is *A–Z Wagon Station*, a work of art that is also a living space. Inside are a mattress and a shelf, and it was created as a living space for the desert in California. The entire front of the *Wagon Station* can flip open. What do you think it would feel like to be inside this piece?
- The artist who created this piece, Andrea Zittel, created a number of these *Wagon Stations*, as well as a number of other pieces reenvisioning how people might live today. She thinks a lot about individual space, human needs, and community. Imagine living in a community in which everyone lived like this. What would work well about that way of living? What problems would people encounter?
- As best you can tell from this artwork and the information I have shared, in what ways do Zittel's ideas about community reflect American founding ideals? In what ways do they challenge these ideals?

Art takes many, sometimes controversial, forms

Grades 5–8; A

- What do you notice about this piece?
- What similarities can you find between this and some other works of art

we have studied this year [for example, Louise Bourgeois's sculpture *Maman*]?

- This work of art is also a living space, and while it was conceived by the artist, Andrea Zittel, it was manufactured in multiples by someone else. If someone were to ask you to explain to them why this is a work of art, what are some answers you might give? Or, why would you claim it is not a work of art?

Camille Pissarro, *The Hermitage at Pontoise* (Plate 14)

Most European (and American) communities are very different now than they were 150 years ago and include technologies that have changed how people live

Grades 3–5; SS

- Take some time and look carefully at this painting. A few minutes later: What do you notice?
- Imagine that we entered this painting. You walk up to the poster, you look at it, and suddenly you are inside this scene, looking around. Notice what you see, hear, smell, feel. What does it feel like to be in this place?
- This was painted in 1867 by the artist Camille Pissarro, and it shows us the French town he lived in, Pontoise. Why might Pissarro have chosen this town to paint over and over? What might Pissarro have wanted to show us about this town?
- Imagine that you could visit this place in the twenty-first century. Knowing how much the world has changed since 1867, how do you think Pontoise might be different today?

Communities have many similarities and differences

Grades 2–5; SS

- What do you notice?
- What can we tell about this place?
- How is this place different from your own community? How is it similar?
- This place, known as the Hermitage, is outside of Pontoise, a town near the city of Paris. The artist lived here for many years. What would it be like to live here?
- Would you want to live here? Why or why not?

Louise Bourgeois, *Maman* (Plate 15)

Artists use symbols as communication tools

Grades 4–8; A, ELA

- What do you notice?
- What words or moods do you associate with this image, and why?
- This sculpture is called *Maman*, which means mother. The artist, Louise Bourgeois, often creates art that symbolizes aspects of her family and childhood. What do you think this sculpture might tell us about her feelings about her mother?

Art is different in different contexts

Grades 3–8; A

- What do you notice?
- In real life, this sculpture is more than 30 feet tall, three times as high as your classroom ceiling. Describe how it would feel to find this sculpture on the sidewalk.
- This sculpture, as you can see in this picture, is outside a museum in an urban area. Artists sometimes place art in specific environments, or even create art for a specific location. How would this sculpture be different in a field?
- If your town bought this piece, where would you put it? Why?

ART INVESTIGATION
METHODOLOGY CHECKLIST

When writing your Art Investigation plan, make sure you . . .

- Determine a theme and a line of inquiry and select a work (or works) that supports this particular inquiry or understanding. Ask a limited number of focused questions that lead students toward consideration of that theme or objective.
- Begin with a question (such as "What do you notice?") that encourages students to carefully observe the work of art first, and follow up with questions that will allow them to interpret what they see.
- Use questions that do not demand a particular answer, elicit a yes or no answer, or contain answers in them.
- Integrate factual information about the work when relevant and available. Know the subject well enough to answer questions when they are asked, but feel comfortable saying "I don't know" to a request for facts.

When leading your Art Investigation, make sure you . . .

- Solicit several responses to each question through wait time and follow-up questions (i.e., "Does anyone have something to add?" "Do others agree/disagree?"). Respond positively to a wide range of responses.
- Spend a significant amount of time at the beginning of the discussion eliciting observations and asking for details about the artwork.
- Ask students to back up their interpretations or assertions with evidence from the artwork.
- Address any student questions or incorrect statements that arise during your inquiry conversation.

You might also want to . . . .

- Call up students' prior knowledge and experiences and ask them to make connections between these ideas and the artwork. Inquire about students' feelings regarding the artwork.
- Design activities and questions for a variety of learning styles, including activities such as writing, drawing, performance, or pair or small-group work; or questions that incorporate other sensory modes (such as "What does this painting sound like?").

FINDING AND WORKING
WITH REPRODUCTIONS

REPRODUCTIONS

Unless you are using Art Investigation Methodology to look at student artwork or your own work, you will be working from reproductions. Some artworks are hard to fully grasp without seeing the original piece. The Guggenheim Museum building is an example of this; the building, with all its wonderful architectural details, cannot be fully represented in one or two images. Installation art (generally a transformation of an entire space, often created for that particular space) is often difficult to understand in reproduction. Film is also difficult to use in an Art Investigation, as it is not visually accessible as a whole at a single moment or during the duration of the conversation. Artworks, as well as the method of presentation in the classroom, should be chosen so that students can best perceive the entire work of art in such a way as to be able to fully grasp or understand that work.

Decide how you are going to share the image with students. What technology is available? Computer projectors and Smart Boards make it easy to use the range of images available on the Internet. Color printers and overhead projectors also allow for use of images from the Web. By using a scanner, you can take a postcard or an image from a book and create a transparency or color copies. If you are scanning, or using a jpg or other type of electronic file, make sure it is of high-enough quality to show or reproduce well in the format you have chosen.

If you do choose to print color reproductions for the class, make sure the image you use is large enough to reproduce without getting pixilated. If it is, we recommend creating a large (11" x 17") color printout. Alternately (or in addition), you might make enough small (8.5" x 11") color printouts for students to look at in pairs, and then have a copy at the front of the room or the discussion area, so that students can have a shared reference point. Better yet, posters are an excellent way to look at images as a class, as they are large, and are generally very high quality. Posters can be purchased from museums or from companies that specialize in creating visual aid resources for educators. Some oversized books and calendars also contain nice, large reproductions, and can sometimes be found at yard sales or used book stores.

Below we have listed some of the Web sites where (as of August 2009) digital images can be found. Museum Web sites are good resources because they often provide some useful information about the artist and/or the artwork along with the image.

USEFUL WEB SITES

The Solomon R. Guggenheim Museum
http://www.guggenheim.org

Guggenheim Collection Online (http://www.guggenheim.org/new-york/collections/collection-online) features artworks indexed by artist, title, date, movement, and material; each artwork includes an image and information about the work. The site also includes two educator resources: Art Curriculum Online (http://www.guggenheim.org/lessons/start/php), which features educator guides from past exhibitions, and the Learning Through Art Web site (http://www.learningthroughart.org), which includes an "Inquiry with Art" section (http://www.learningthroughart.org/inquiry art.php) that allows you to watch, find, or create an Art Investigation plan.

Art:21
http://www.pbs.org/art21/index.html

The PBS series *Art: 21* focuses exclusively on twenty-first century artists, with an image-rich Artwork Survey available online for each artist featured; episodes are centered around themes. Videos and lesson plans, including curriculum tie-ins, are also available online.

ArtsConnectEd
http://artsconnected.org

ArtsConnectEd brings together images from the Walker Art Center and the Minneapolis Institute of Arts. Search through the collections by keyword, artist name, culture, or medium.

Artcyclopedia
http://www.artcyclopedia.com

There are no images on this site, but you can search for artists by various categories, and there will be links to other sites that have works by each artist.

The Art Institute of Chicago
http://www.artic.edu/aic/collections/

The online collection of the Museum of the Art Institute of Chicago includes a large database of images searchable by keyword, artist, or culture; theme explorations are also available.

Freer and Sackler Gallery, Smithsonian Institution
http://www.asia.si.edu/collections/default.htm

This Web site offers images and information from all areas of the museum's collection, which specializes in art from all over Asia, including Chinese, Japanese, Korean, Southeast Asian, and South Asian and Himalayan art.

Google Image Search
http://images.google.com/

This search engine functions exactly like a Google Web search but produces only image results; search by artist name, artistic movement, or any other search term you can formulate.

The Metropolitan Museum of Art
http://www.metmuseum.org

The Metropolitan Museum of Art's Web site has a searchable online Collection Database, which contains descriptions and often images of art works; click on "Advanced Search" to search by artist, medium, and other categories.

Museum of Fine Arts, Boston
http://educators.mfa.org/home/

The Educators Online tool from the Museum of Fine Arts, Boston, allows you to create your own gallery online from the Museum's collections using a variety of search methods; you can also view galleries created by other educators.

National Museum of African Art, Smithsonian Institution
http://africa.si.edu/collections/index.htm

This collection of African art can be searched by classification, use, region, country, ethnic group, or artist, and includes both traditional and contemporary art.

National Museum of the American Indian
http://www.nmai.si.edu/searchcollections/home.aspx

The collection can be searched by peoples/cultures, artists/individuals, places, or specific objects, and includes an interactive map that allows you to search a region or a specific people.

The Tate Gallery
http://www.tate.org.uk/collection/

Search the Tate Gallery's collection online by artist name or artwork title, or browse by subjects as various as history, nature, and work and occupations.

Web Gallery of Art
http://www.wga.hu

Featuring European painting and sculpture, the Web Gallery of Art Web site is searchable by artist name, time period, and other terms; the Dual Mode feature allows you to place two separate images side by side on the same Web page.

The Whitney Museum of American Art
www.whitney.org/learning

The Web site for the Whitney Museum of American Art features a teacher section. Highlights include a gallery area in which artworks are grouped by theme, style, and other categories; a research section filled with learning resources; and a Collect Art section where you can gather images from the online gallery and turn the collection into a slide show or send as an e-mail.

NOTES

Chapter 1

1. For example, Visual Thinking Strategies, developed by Phillip Yenowine and Abigail Housen; for more information see http://www.vtshome.org.

2. For example, museum educators Rika Burnham and Elliot Kai-Kee. See their article "The Art of Teaching in the Museum," *Journal of Aesthetic Education, 39*(1).

Chapter 4

1. For a similar list of artists' processes, or "studio habits of mind," see Lois Hetland, Ellen Winner, Shirley Veenema, and Kimberly M. Sheridan, *Studio Thinking: The Real Benefits of Visual Arts Education* (New York: Teachers College Press, 2007).

Chapter 6

1. This research was funded by the U.S. Department of Education's Office of Innovation and Improvement, through their "Arts Education Model Development and Dissemination" funding stream.

BIBLIOGRAPHY

Art: 21. (n.d.) *Cai Guo-Qiang: Biography.* Retrieved May 25, 2009, from http://www.pbs.org/art21/artists/cai/index.html#.

Barr, A. H. (1951). *Matisse: His art and his public.* New York: The Museum of Modern Art.

Barrett, T. (2003). *Interpreting art: Reflecting, wondering, and responding.* New York: McGraw-Hill.

Baxandall, M. (1988). *Painting & experience in fifteenth-century Italy.* New York: Oxford University Press.

Blessing, J. (2009). *Kiki Smith, Ribs.* Retrieved January 31, 2009, from Guggenheim Collection Online: http://www.guggenheim.org/new-york/collections/collection-online/show-full/piece/?search=Kiki%20 Smith&page=1&f=People&cr=1.

Blessing, J. (2009). *Mark Chagall, Paris Through the Window.* Retrieved January 31, 2009, from Guggenheim Collection Online: http://www.guggenheim.org/new-york/collections/collection-online/show-full/piece/?search=Marc%20 Chagall&page=1&f=People&cr=3

Bloch, S. (1976). An interview with Louise Bourgeois. *Art Journal, 35*(4), 370–373. Retrieved January 10, 2009, from http://www.jstor.org/stable/776230

Bresler, L. (1995). The subservient, co-equal, affective, and social integration styles and their implications for the arts. *Arts Education Policy Review, 96* (5), 31–38. Retrieved January 10, 2009, from Academic Search Premier, EBSCOhost .

Burn, B. (1993). *Masterpieces of the Metropolitan Museum of Art.* New York: Little, Brown.

Burnham, R., & Kai-Kee, E. (2005). The art of teaching in the museum. *Journal of Aesthetic Education, 39*(1), 65–76.

Caillies, S., Denhière, G., & Kintsch, W. (2002). The effect of prior knowledge on understanding from text: Evidence from primed recognition. *European Journal of Cognitive Psychology,* 14(2), 267–286.

California Department of Education. (n.d.). Vocabulary development. In *Taking Center Stage—Act II (TCSII): A portal for middle grades educators.* Retrieved July 9, 2008, from http://pubs.cde.ca.gov/tcsii/ch1/vocabdev.aspx

Calkins, L. M. (2001). *The art of teaching reading.* New York: Longman.

Collins, B. R. (1991). What is art history? *Art Education, 44*(1), 53–59. Retrieved

January 10, 2009, from http://www.jstor.org/stable/3193265

Edwards, T. (1915). *A dictionary of thoughts: A cyclopedia of laconic quotations.* Detroit: F.B. Dickerson.

Eisner, E. (2002) *The arts and the creation of mind.* New Haven, CT: Yale University Press.

Eliot, G. (1963). The natural history of German life. In T. Pinney (Ed.), *Essays of George Eliot.* New York: Columbia University Press. (Original work published 1856)

Felton, M. K., & Kuhn, D. (2007). "How do I know?" The epistemological roots of critical thinking. *Journal of Museum Education, 32*(2), 101–110.

Greene, M. (2001). *Variations on a blue guitar.* New York: Teachers College Press.

Solomon R. Guggenheim Museum. (2009). Guggenheim: Collection Online. Retrieved January 31, 2009, from http://www.guggenheim.org/new-york/collections/collection-online

Guterman, N. (1963) *A book of French quotations.* New York: Doubleday.

Harrison, C., & Wood, P. (1999). *Art in theory, 1900–1990: An anthology of changing ideas.* Malden, MA: Blackwell.

Hetland, L., Winner, E., Veenema, S., & Sheridan, K. M. (2007). *Studio thinking: The real benefits of visual arts education.* New York: Teachers College Press.

Hirsh, E. D. (2006). Why the absence of a content-rich curriculum core hurts poor children most. *American Educator, 30*(1). Retrieved July 3, 2008, from http://www.aft.org/pubs-reports/american_educator/issues/spring06/PoorChildren.pdf

Institute for Learning Innovation (Adams, M., Foutz, S., Luke, J., & Stein, J.). (2007). *Thinking through art: Isabella Stewart Gardner Museum School Partnership Program: Year 3 Research Results.* Retrieved January 30, 2009, from the Isabella Stewart Gardner Museum Web site: http://www.gardnermuseum.org/education/tta/links/Year_3_Report.pdf

Keene, E. O., & Zimmermann, S. (1997). *Mosaic of thought: Teaching comprehension in a reader's workshop.* Portsmouth, NH: Heinemann.

Kuhn, D. (2005). *Education for thinking.* Cambridge, MA: Harvard University Press.

Maine, B. (1999). Erich Auerbach's "Mimesis" and Nelson Goodman's "Ways of Worldmaking": A nominal(ist) revision. *Poetics Today, 20*(1), 41–52. Retrieved January 10, 2009, from http://www.jstor.org/stable/1773342

Perkins, D. (1994). *The intelligent eye.* Los Angeles: J. Paul Getty Trust.

Project Zero (with Tishman, S.). (1999). Investigating the educational impact and potential of the Museum of Modern Art's visual thinking curriculum. Cambridge, MA: Project Zero, Harvard Graduate School of Education.

Randi Korn & Associates. (2007). Teaching literacy through art: Final report: Synthesis of 2004–5 and 2005–6 studies. Retrieved January 30, 2009, from http://www.learningthroughart.org/pdfs/Final_Distribution_RKA_2007_Guggenheim_TLTA_report.pdf

Rawlinson, K., Wood, S. N., Osterman, M., & Sullivan, C. (2007). Thinking critically about social issues through visual materials. *Journal of Museum Education, 30*(2), 155–174.

Ritchie, M. (n.d.). *Information, cells, and evil.* Interview with Matthew Ritchie by Art:21. Retrieved May 25, 2009, from Art:21–Art in the Twenty-First Century Web site: http://www.pbs.org/art21/artists/ritchie/clip1.html

Rodman, S. (1957). *Conversations with artists.* New York: Devin-Adair.

Rosenshine, B., Meister, C., & Chapman, S. (1996). Teaching students to generate questions: A review of the intervention studies. *Review of Educational Research, 66*(2), 181–221.

Rufino Tamayo. (2009). In *Encyclopedia Britannica.* Retrieved May 25, 2009, from Encyclopedia Britannica Online: http://www.britannica.com/EBchecked/topic/581853/Rufino-Tamayo

Runco, M. (2007). *Creativity: Theories and themes: Research, development, and practice.* San Diego, CA: Elsevier Academic Press.

Schmidt, L. (2004). *Classroom confidential: The 12 secrets of great teachers.* Portsmouth, NH: Heinemann.

Shaull, R. (1997). Introduction. In P. Freire, *Pedagogy of the oppressed.* New York: Continuum.

Simpson's contemporary quotations. (1988). Boston: Houghton Mifflin. Retrieved January 28, 2009, Credo Reference, from at http://corp.credoreference.com

Solis, F. (2004) *The Aztec empire: Catalogue of the exhibition.* New York: Guggenheim Museum.

Spector, N. (2009). *Vasily Kandinsky, Composition 8.* Retrieved May 25, 2009, from Guggenheim Collection Online: http://www.guggenheim.org/new-york/collections/collection-online/show-full/piece/?search=Vasily%20Kandinsky&page=2&f=People&cr=10

Tobin, K. (1987). The role of wait time in higher cognitive level learning. *Review of Educational Research, 57*(1), 69–95. Retrieved January 10, 2009, from http://www.jstor.org/stable/1170357

Tough, P. (2006, November 26). What it takes to make a student. *New York Times Magazine.* Retrieved July 3, 2000, from http://www.nytimes.com/2006/11/26/magazine/26tough.html?pagewanted=print

Walker, K. (n.d.). *Projecting fictions: "Insurrection! Our tools were rudimentary, yet we pressed on."* Interview with Kara Walker by Art:21. Retrieved May 25, 2009, from *Art:21*–Art in the Twenty-First Century Web site: http://www.pbs.org/art21/artists/walker/clip1.html

Wiggins, G., & McTighe, J. (1998). *Understanding by design.* Alexandria, VA: Association for Supervision and Curriculum Development.

Willingham, D. T. (2003). Students remember . . . what they think about. *American Educator, 27*(2), 37–41. Retrieved July 3, 2008, from http://www.aft.org/pubs-reports/american_educator/summer2003/cogsci.html

Willingham, D. T. (2006). How knowledge helps. *American Educator, 30*(1), 30–37. Retrieved July 3, 2008, from http://www.aft.org/pubs-reports/american_educator/issues/spring06/willingham.htm

Willingham, D. T. (2007). Critical thinking: Why is it so hard to teach? *American Educator, 31*(2), 11–19. Retrieved July 3, 2008, from http://www.aft.org/pubs-reports/american_educator/issues/summer07/Crit_Thinking.pdf

Zittel, A. (n.d.). Andrea Zittel's a–z. Retrieved May 25, 2009, from http://www.zittel.org/

CREDITS

Grateful acknowledgment is made for permission to reproduce the following:

Louise Bourgeois, *Maman*, 1999: Art © Louise Bourgeois/Licensed by VAGA, New York, NY.

Cai Guo-Qiang, *The Vague Border at the Edge of Time/Space Project*, 1991: © Cai Guo-Qiang. Photograph by André Morin.

Marc Chagall, *Paris through the Window* and *Green Violinist:* © 2009 Artists Right Society (ARS), New York/ADAGP, Paris.

Rineke Dijkstra, *Coney Island, N.Y., USA, July 9, 1993* (from the *Beaches* series), 1993: © Rineke Dijkstra and Marian Goodman Gallery, New York.

Arshile Gorky, *Untitled:* © 2009 Artists Rights Society (ARS), New York.

Ann Hamilton, *untitled (the capacity of absorption)*, 1988/93: © Ann Hamilton.

Roni Horn, *Still Water (The River Thames, for Example)*, 1999 (detail): © Tate, London, 2009.

Wassily Kandinsky, *Composition 8* and *Blue Mountain:* © 2009 Artists Right Society (ARS), New York/ADAGP, Paris.

Joan Miró, *Landscape (the Hare)*, 1927: © 2009 Successió Miró/Artists Rights Society (ARS), New York/ADAGP, Paris.

Cindy Sherman, *Untitled Film Still, #15*, 1978: Courtesy of the Artist and Metro Studios.

Rufino Tamayo, *Heavenly Bodies*, 1946: © D.R. Rufino Tamayo/Herederos/Mexico/2009. Fundación Olga y Rufino Tamayo, A.C.

Treasure Box (Papahou): The Metropolitan Museum of Art, The Michael C. Rockefeller Memorial Collection. Purchase, Nelson A. Rockefeller, 1960 (1978.412.755a, b). Image © The Metropolitan Museum of Art

Jamie Wefald, *Untitled*, 2007: © Jamie Wefald.

Andrea Zittel, *A–Z Wagon Station customized by Russell Whitten*, 2003: © Andrea Zittel.

ABOUT THE AUTHOR

Rebecca Shulman Herz has managed the Solomon R. Guggenheim Museum's Learning Through Art program since 2000. She has led numerous workshops about facilitating conversations around works of art for classroom teachers, art educators, and museum educators. Her previous publications include articles (*Journal of Museum Education*) and short fiction (*Quarto*). Prior to joing the Guggenheim Museum she worked for an after-school program focused on creative writing and literacy.

Special Offer

Purchase five or more posters
from the Guggenheim Online Store
and receive a 50% discount.

http://www.guggenheimstore.org/
Enter code POST5 at checkout.
Offer good through December 31, 2010.